Sprirtual Qi Gong

Spiritual Qi Gong

A practical Taoist Manual for Health, Longevity and Self-Realization!

David Twicken, Ph.D., L.Ac.

Authors Choice
San Jose New York Lincoln Shanghai

Spiritual Qi Gong
A practical Taoist Manual for Health, Longevity and Self-Realization!

Authors Choice Press
an imprint of iUniverse.com, Inc.

For information address:
iUniverse.com, Inc.
5220 S 16th, Ste. 200
Lincoln, NE 68512
www.iuniverse.com

ISBN: 0-595-17497-3

Printed in the United States of America

Disclaimer

The information in this book is based on the author's knowledge and personal experience. It is presented for educational purposes to assist the reader in expanding their knowledge of Asian philosophy and Qi Gong. Before using any of the techniques in this book consult a licensed physician for advice on whether or not to practice them. The techniques and practices are to be used at the reader's own discretion and liability. The author is not responsible in any manner whatsoever for any injury that may occur by following the instructions in this book.

Acknowledgments

During the past twenty five years I have had the opportunity to meet some unique people that have influenced my life, each in their special way have inspired me to learn and share ancient Asian knowledge. I would like to thank and acknowledge Maezumi Roshi, Gary Lam, Huang Chi Ni, Dr. Huang, Mary Chow, Daniel Lee, Hawkins Cheung, Tim O'Connor, Larry Sang, Joseph Yu, Virginia Bailey, Michael Hamilton, Michael Winn, Gregory Leblanc, Lin Yun and special thanks to Mr. Mantak Chia for teaching alchemy to all with the desire to learn and the Universal Tao Center for allowing me to use photographs in this book. Special thanks to my uncle Harris, one of the most extraordinary and generous people I have ever known; my aunt Linda, a living example of unconditional love and compassion; my aunt Bernice, who was there when I needed her most and my brother Larry, who has always supported me throughout my life.

Author Contact:
www.chineseastrologynow.com

Table of Contents

About this book xi
Introduction xiii
Universal Cosmology 3
Life Force and Yin Yang 11
Five Elements 15
Five Element Organ Rejuvenation 37
Heavenly Orbit Qi Gong 47
Five Elements and Five Shen 55
Eight Treasures Qi Gong 63
Shen-Spirit Realization 77
Navel Tan Tien Center 80
Solar Plexus Tan Tien Center 82
Heart Tan Tien Center 85
Third Eye Tan Tien Center 87
Conclusion 90
Appendix 91
Introduction to the Chinese Calendar 93
Chinese Calendar 97

About this book

Spiritual Qi Gong reveals the ancient Taoist system of internal alchemy for Health, Longevity and Spiritual Development. The practices contained in this book have been kept a closely guarded secret for centuries. Taoist internal alchemy or spiritual cultivation has historically been written in ambiguous and obtuse forms, primarily to retain the true meaning from being revealed to the public. My primary objective in writing this book is to communicate these ancient meditations in an easily understandable method. The benefits obtained from these practices include emotional harmony, physical health, vitality, longevity and spiritual development.

The information presented is the result of thousands of years of human spiritual development; it is derived from ancient Taoist cannons, which are esoteric books explaining Asian Arts. The following texts are the basis of this book: Tai Hsuan (Great Mystery) and Hui Ming Ching (Uniting Mind and Vitality). The alchemical formulas in this book are the Five Elements Organ Rejuvenation, Heavenly Orbit, Eight Treasures, Shen-Spirit Realization (Kan and Li transformations of the Navel, Solar Plexus, Heart and Third Eye centers). The presentation of this material is based on my twenty-five years of studying, practicing and teaching Asian arts; I have retained the essence of the traditional practices while presenting them in a clear, easily understandable format for modern society. People of all philosophical, spiritual or educational backgrounds can practice these meditations; it is a path that reveals spiritual truth common to all human life.

The Appendix includes the Chinese Calendar and procedures for calculating the five element energy for any hour, day, month or year. This information identifies nature's five element energies; it allows the opportunity to develop the sensitivity to perceive which elements are favorable or unfavorable to your health and spiritual cultivation. One benefit of this knowledge is it allows you to develop a Qi Gong plan that obtains harmony among the five elements generated from nature's cycles of time.

A key element within Spiritual Qi Gong is human life is an integrated whole. Human life consists of three major influences: Physical, Mental and Spiritual, they are one undivided whole. Each type of Qi Gong affects all aspects of life, while some may focus more on one area than another, all aspects of life are affected by these practices. There are common experiences for all people who practice these meditations, but each person is unique and may experience different levels and depths. Additionally, each practice is connected to every other practice, often activating or stimulating an experience explained in another Qi Gong section, this is normal and an example of the integration of human life. Follow the practices in a gentle and relaxed way and you will taste the fruit of Spiritual Qi Gong.

Introduction

It was a cold winter night in New Hampshire, starring out my bedroom window the Moon and Stars beautifully illuminated the sky, they radiated deep inside my spirit; intuitively I knew answers to my questions would come from these magnificent life forms. It is three decades later and that day remains so very vivid, the intensity of questioning the meaning and purpose of my life seems as clear as if it was yesterday. This desire to understand the meaning of life can be found in cultures throughout the world, they have developed practices, techniques, philosophies and religions that reveal the relationship between human life and the creator of all life. In ancient China, a system of spiritual cultivation evolved, "Spiritual Qi Gong", which comprises numerous styles of meditations. The ancients developed these practices with the goal of achieving physical, mental and spiritual development. Spiritual Qi Gong practices lead to realizing the immortal nature of human spirit. They are gentle, energetic meditations that guide internal and universal energies, including Earth, Sun, Moon, North Star, Big Dipper and Starry Beings throughout one's body, transforming emotional, physical and spiritual consciousness. These ancient people understood immortality to be the conscious unification of human life with the original source of life. These ancients directly experienced the fruits of these practices and are examples that this "unification" can be experienced during a lifetime.

There is one requirement to obtain the fruit of Spiritual Qi Gong, a person must be virtuous; without virtue the fruit of this work cannot be achieved. Virtue is a magnet that attracts energies necessary to refine and cultivate body, mind and spirit. These practices begin a process of refinement and transformation; the key is to relax and have an open, virtuous heart, as you practice the fruit will appear.

Taoist internal alchemy consists of transforming Jing into Qi and Qi into Shen. Jing is essence, the base energy of life; it can also be called biological or reproductive energy. Qi is vitality or life force and Shen is Spirit. These three aspects of life are referred to as the "Three Treasures". Jing or essence is the densest and most physical of the three, it is the foundation for the two other treasures. Qi is created from the transformation of Jing, and Qi nourishes Shen. They are one undivided whole. This transformation process occurs naturally. Stress, tension, emotional and mental disharmony can slow, block or cause an imbalance among the Three Treasures, for instance, to much emphasis can be placed on material or sexual interests, this causes one's life force to be directed towards those areas of life and away from the natural transformation and evolution towards spiritual growth. Spiritual Qi Gong gently guides transformation of Jing to Qi and Qi to spiritual consciousness and development. These practices restore the natural rhythm of life, the foundation supporting spirit.

A new life consists of the coupling or blending of the essences of man and woman; the Jing, Qi and Shen of parents act as a magnet, attracting a Shen-Spirit to take human form. In Taoist internal alchemy, the process of transforming Jing into Qi is enhanced during Qi Gong practices, these ancient meditations are performed in the Tan Tien, the spiritual womb contained by each human. Qi Gong or alchemical practices refine Jing, Qi and Shen, initiating conscious awareness of one's eternal nature. With time and cultivation, one's refined energy attracts the "Immortal Pill" or "Heavenly Elixir", the fruit of this practice. Receiving the Immortal Pill is the subtle realm, Tao or God delivering the divine spirit to your spiritual womb, combining vitality and consciousness, creating an immortal body; that is the traditional way of explaining this alchemy. A modern explanation would be Spiritual Qi Gong is the process of refining one's thoughts, actions and conscious understanding of the integrated, eternal nature of life. In other words, it is refining one's consciousness by cultivating person vitality and the collective vitality of the Universe, leading to the direct realization of one's true nature. This is the ancient method of immortality revealed in this book.

Chapter 1

Universal Cosmology

The Universe is a self-generating, multi-dimensional, eternal evolving entity. One integral principle that permeates the Universe is "root always exists within a branch"; this root to branch relationship is the basis of Spiritual Qi Gong. One application of this root to branch interaction is explained by the ancient Chinese symbol Tai Chi (Figure 1a). Tai Chi consists of a trinity: pre-heaven or Yang, post-heaven or Yin and the integration of the two, Tai Chi. The pre-heaven condition is life before time, space and the dimension of duality, it is an eternal, self-generating, undivided unity. The post-heaven stage is the stage of transformation; it is reflected by the principles of Yin-Yang, and the physical, dual world. The dimensions of polarity: time and space, form this post-heaven condition and the interaction of pre-heaven and post-heaven energies create human life or Tai Chi, these three aspects of life exist simultaneously, they are one undivided whole. Spiritual Qi Gong is designed to guide a person to realize the unity of pre-heaven and post-heaven life, revealing their true spiritual nature.

Pre-heaven or subtle realm is referred to as the Mysterious Mother; like a Mother, it gives birth to life. The subtle realm includes pure, undivided energy; it is the destination or fruit of Spiritual Qi Gong. The process of "connecting" to the subtle realm begins with the unification of the physical, emotional, energetic and spiritual bodies. This unification process expands a person's awareness of the subtle realm, allowing one to experience it in daily life.

The subtle realm is the pre-heaven or Godly realm and the root of life; it is also the vitality contained within all branches of life. Post-heaven includes branches of the subtle realm; they are direct extensions of the subtle realm and comprise the manifest, dual world. Branches are always connected to root, it is within these branches Spiritual Qi Gong reconnects a person to the source of life; branches are the pathways to root, subtle realm or God. From a Universal perspective, the root and branch are one, undivided reality and this realization and experience is the fruit of Spiritual Qi Gong. The subtle realm, the original, undivided state expanded itself to create all life, it is through these life forms or branches that Spiritual Qi Gong deepens the connection and understanding between human life and the subtle realm. This process guides, grows and harvests human consciousness into a mature immortal spirit. The following section explains aspects of the unmanifest and manifest realms, Diagram 1a illustrates these relationships.

- The first expression or branch of the subtle realm includes *Immortal Divine Beings*; they are pure spirits and fully God conscious. They are guides for humans and the source of Spiritual Qi Gong.
- The second expression or branch includes *Solar Beings or Natural Deities*, they are locations in the Universe that gather and store subtle energy. This category of life includes Stars and Planets, which are transmitters for receiving and distributing pure, unaltered energy of the Subtle Realm. These living entities are centers of energy that humans can develop relationships, acting as pathways that guide aspiring humans to the subtle realm or God consciousness. Solar Beings or Natural Deities act as spiritual compasses, guiding human life to their final destination. Human life benefits by connecting, communicating and absorbing their energy, nourishing and revitalizing human consciousness, providing energy and guidance for spiritual evolution.
- Immortal Spirits are another expression of the subtle realm. Immortality is a state of consciousness or awareness of the Subtle Realm; human life has the opportunity to cultivate and refine themselves to become an Immortal or aware of their true nature. In this awareness, time and space or the polar dimension is transcended and one merges with the undivided, original, subtle

realm. An Immortal, at will, enters and exits the Manifest and Unmanifest dimensions; in reality, for an Immortal, there is no difference between the Unmanifest and Manifest, they are one undivided whole.

Figure 1a

Diagram 1a

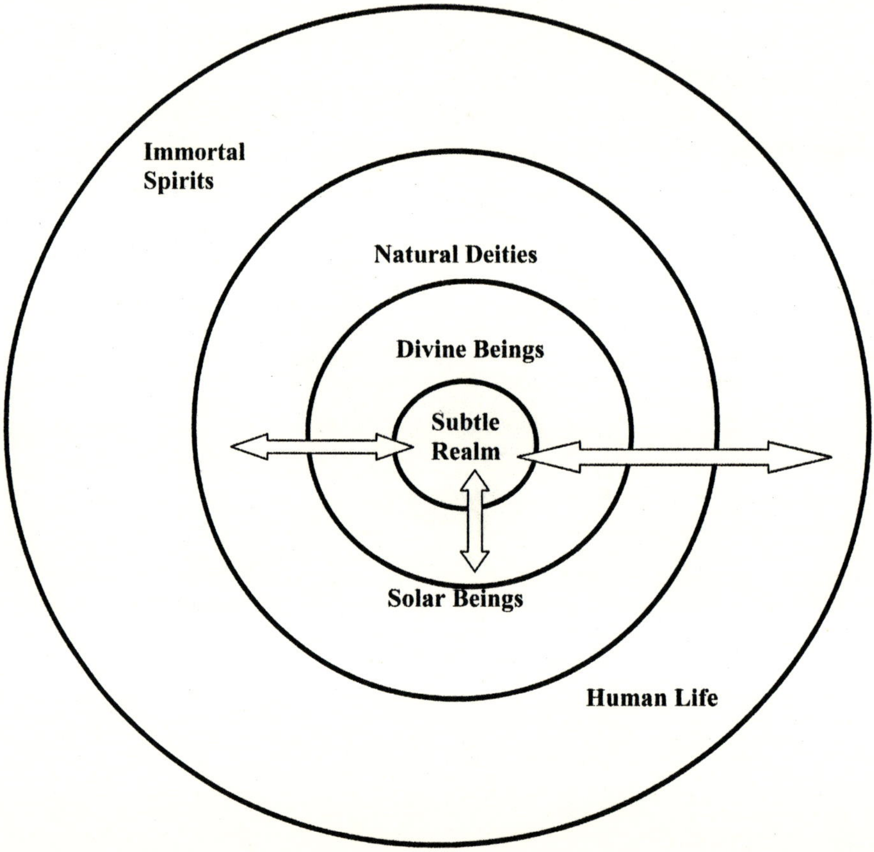

In the same way man and woman "couple" to create new life, Spiritual Qi Gong is an energetic mirror of that process. Alchemical Spiritual Qi Gong practices blend energies of stars, planets and cosmic forces with human life, this "blending" gives "birth" to an Immortal Spirit. It is a spiritual birth mirroring the Universal birth of human life. Within each person is a "spiritual womb" or Tan Tien; this womb contains internal and external energies to be blended and refined, transforming a person. This transformation process not only purifies one's emotional, physical and spiritual energy, but also connects to Universal energies that unify individual spirit with the subtle realm. It is the result of this refinement and purification process human consciousness transcends post-natal influences and unites with the pre-natal stage, this process reveals the Immortal Spirit within each person. This is the secret. The secret within the secret is that we have always and will always be this Immortal Spirit, the alchemical formulas or practices are designed to allow a person to ***realize*** or become ***conscious*** of this aspect of their life. Realizing and experiencing immortality is more than a spiritual rebirth, which can be just a glimpse of their true nature; it includes retaining this achievement and incorporating it into daily life.

One goal of Spiritual Qi Gong is realizing that pre-heaven and post-heaven life exist simultaneously, this reality is why humans can experience the Subtle Realm in this life, we do not have to wait for another life. These ancient Qi Gong practices assist in the evolution of human consciousness and removes the veil people wear, not only revealing their true spiritual nature, but causing a permanent transformation into a new dimension of awareness. This dimension is represented by the Tai Chi symbol, the integration of pre-heaven and post-heaven life, in essence, realizing Heaven within Earth.

Spirit is a direct expression of the Subtle Realm, it can be viewed in two major ways. The first is viewing Spirit in a maco way, as an integrated, eternal or immortal aspect of subtle spiritual energy in human form. The second way of viewing spirit is viewing components of Human Form as "Spirits". The underlying and permeating principle is that the subtle realm exists within every living component in the Universe. Spiritual Qi Gong is based on this truth and consists of methods to enhance experiencing unity with the source of life, Tao or God.

The human body is a living being and each element of the body, ranging from cells to internal organs, contribute towards maintaining life. The Heart, Lungs, Spleen, Liver and Kidneys are living components within the body; their functioning must be sustained to properly maintain a healthy life. These organs have a life force and can be viewed as a branch of the eternal Spirit within the body; the ancients viewed these organs as spirits within the body because they contribute towards maintaining life. The energy branches of the subtle realm: planets, stars, food and water vitalize human life and its organ system; the Chinese choose to call these Universal energies contained in the organs "Spirits". Their understanding is these "Spirits" are a life force; they are branches from the subtle realm, similar to the relationship of limbs to the trunk of a body. Each person has a "big spirit" and "small" spirits; the "big" spirit is the composite or integration of all "spirits" or energies of the body, the "small" spirits are the centers, expressions or components of the "big" spirit. From an alchemy viewpoint, each aspect or branch of life contains root; every microcosm contains the root of the Universe, this reality is the basis of Spiritual Qi Gong.

Chapter 2

Life Force and Yin Yang

The ancient Asian cosmological view is that the Universe is filled with an energy that flows through infinite cycles of transformation. This energy comprises all of life; including stars, planets, trees, mountains, water, animals and human life, this energy is referred to as Qi. Qi is both energy and matter, as well as the force that allows the transformation from energy to matter and matter to energy. For example, Water is a type of Qi and is a perfect example of how Qi transforms. Water can be in the form of ice; ice can transform into Water and Water into steam. Qi is ice, Qi is Water, Qi is steam and Qi is the heat that allows the transformation to occur. Qi is all of life. Every part of the Universe is a blend of different types of Qi. To understand this blending of Qi is to understand life. Knowing the rhythms and expressions of Qi is the basis for Spiritual Qi Gong and transforming life.

The human body is comprised of Qi. Bones, tendons and muscles are dense forms of Qi. Blood and energy are subtler forms of Qi; spirit is the subtlest form of Qi. Cycles of growth are examples of different ways Qi moves or unfolds. The transformation from infancy to childhood, childhood to adolescence and adolescence to adulthood is slow and gradual. This process reflects one way Qi unfolds. Another process can be explained by exercising muscles. Exercising muscles causes quick changes in strength and shape. Natural transformations cannot be altered to make an infant become a child faster. The inherit unfolding of this Qi process is very different than the quick development of exercising muscles. Some forms of Qi are slow, others fast, knowing the influences of Qi is the foundation for developing an effective system to manage Qi and health. The natural transformations of water and human growth are examples of transformation; spiritual transformation is a blend of unconscious and conscious transformation. Alchemy consists of gathering, circulating, refining and integrating internal and external energies, this transformation process will occur differently for each person, the fruits will be the same, the time and challenges may differ. Unlike natural human development, spiritual transformation includes conscious effort, Spiritual Qi Gong is an ancient path of unconscious and conscious Qi transformation.

In China, a model of understanding nature evolved which would become the root of Chinese philosophy, Medicine, Nutrition, Martial Arts, Feng Shui, Astrology and Spiritual Alchemy. This system is Yin-Yang. Yin-Yang theory includes viewing the Universe as one integrated whole, as well as two opposing, but interdependent elements. All aspects of life can be categorized into Yin-Yang. For example, Heaven-Earth, Man-Woman, Hot-Cold, Left-Right, Light-Dark, Front-Back, Hard-Soft, North-South, East-West, Root-Branch, Top-Bottom and Fast-Slow are different sides of one phenomenon. Yin-Yang theory categories any situation into two aspects, each aspect is inseparable from its opposite. There must be a Left to have a Right, a Strong to have a Weak, a Front to have a Back, they are not two separate entities; they are two sides of the same phenomenon.

Yin-Yang is a predominant component in spiritual cultivation and alchemy. One major application of Yin-Yang theory is that Yang represents a growing or expanding phase, and Yin, a declining phase. All of life flows through this basic model of waxing and waning. Each expansion leads to a decline, which leads to another expansion and another decline, in an endless cycle. Internal organs and vital substances (Qi, Blood, Body Fluids, Essence) will be Yang-excess, Yin-deficient or balanced. In spiritual cultivation and alchemy, determining the condition of each organ and emotion, whether derived constitutionally or by way of lifestyle, provides a tool to enhance the effectiveness of cultivation.

Chapter 3

Five Elements

The Five Elements are an integral aspect of Asian arts. They are the ABC's of calculating, evaluating and applying knowledge of Spiritual Qi Gong, Chinese astrology and Feng Shui. The following explains the Five Elements.

This circle is an integrated whole. It represents the oneness of life.

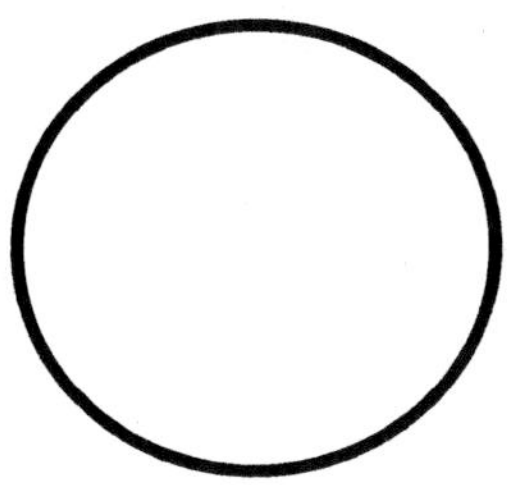

A circle can also be viewed as two parts, the top is Yang and the bottom is Yin.

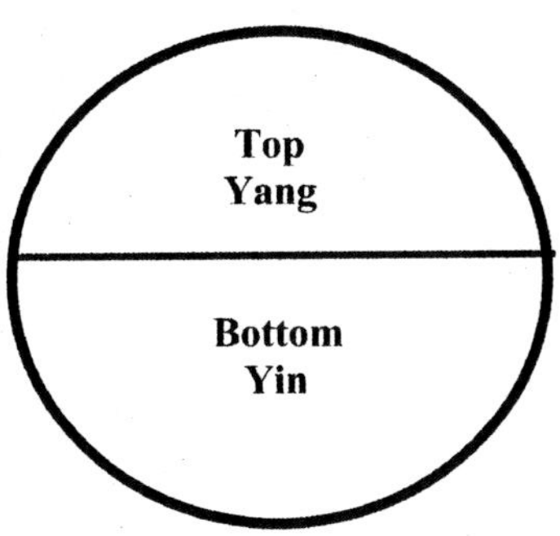

This same circle can be viewed with five phases, the Five Elements.

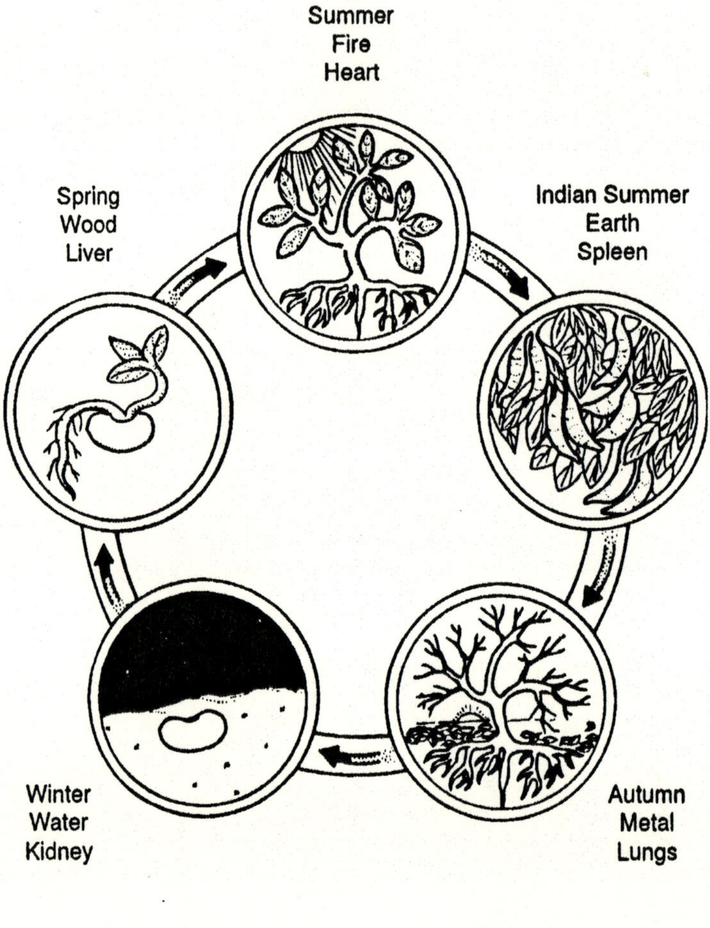

Each area or phase is assigned an element: Water, Wood, Fire, Earth and Metal. For example, Wood is positioned where the circle begins to move upward and represents growth or Springtime; Fire is located where the portion of the circle reaches its peak, symbolizing Summer; Earth is positioned where harvesting takes place, representing Indian Summer; Metal represents turning inward or contraction, representing Autumn, and Water is where the circle turns completely inward to regenerate, representing Winter. Water also portrays preparation for a new Spring, Wood or growth cycle. This cycle continues infinitely and reflects self-generation and the eternal nature of life.

The relative position of each of the Five Elements or Five Phases in the circle determines its specific relationship with every other element. For example, Water is the mother to Wood, grandparent to Fire, grandchild of Earth and child of Metal. Each element has those distinct relationships with the four remaining elements. The ability to apply those relationships is crucial to all Asian arts. Table 3a summarizes these relationships.

Table 3a

Element ⟶	Water	Wood	Fire	Earth	Metal
Parent	Metal	Water	Wood	Fire	Earth
Sibling—Same	Water	Wood	Fire	Earth	Metal
Child – Offspring	Wood	Fire	Earth	Metal	Water
Grandchild	Fire	Earth	Metal	Water	Wood
Grandparent Controller	Earth	Metal	Water	Wood	Fire

Interpreting this chart.

Water's parent is Metal.
Water's sibling is Water.
Water's child is Wood.
Water's grandchild is Fire.
Water's Controller is Earth.

From these relationships we see five key interactions.

1. Each element gives to another element, the parent.
2. Each element controls another element, the grandparent or controller.

3. Each element is controlled by another element, the grandchild.
4. Each element receives from another element, the child.
5. Each element is supported by another element, the same or sibling.

These relationships are expressed in the actions of giving, receiving, controlling and being controlled. Obtaining a natural healthy life depends on finding balance within these five interactions. One action is not better than another, there is only meaning when a situation is compared to a particular birth chart. What is beneficial is relative to the condition of all elements in the Four Pillars. Each of the relationships can be balanced, excessive, or deficient. Four Pillars is a tool that reveals how the Universe created a Five Elements combination at birth.

Table 3b

Situation	First Action	Second Action
Weakness	Nourish. Add the Parent Element. Add same – Sibling element.	Add a small amount of the Grandparent element to make the Parent stronger when appropriate.
Too Strong or Excessive	Control. Add the Grandparent.	Reduce. Add the Child element to drain the overly strong parent.

The following diagrams illustrate how each element is affected by all elements. Determine which elements are needed when an excessive or weakness exists. Confirm your choices with Table 3c below.

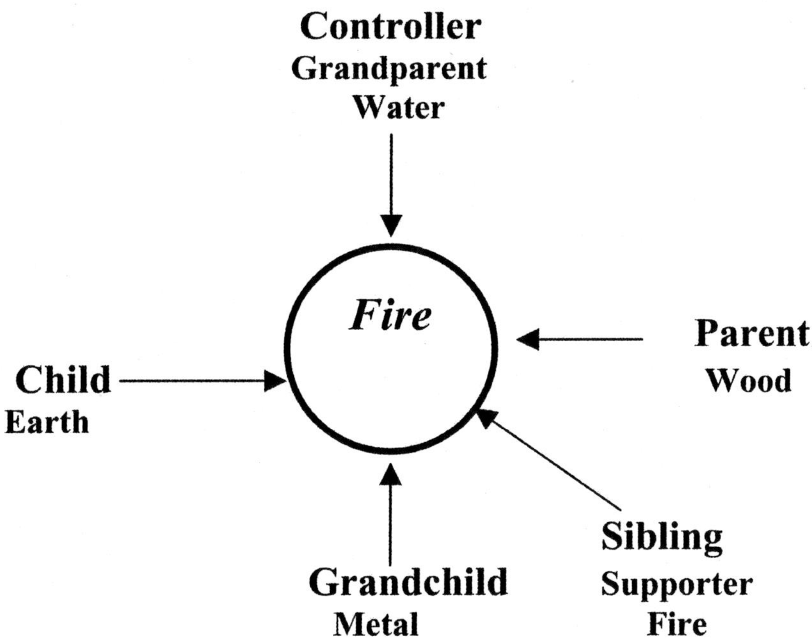
Controller
Grandparent
Water
Fire
Parent
Wood
Child
Earth
Sibling
Supporter
Fire
Grandchild
Metal

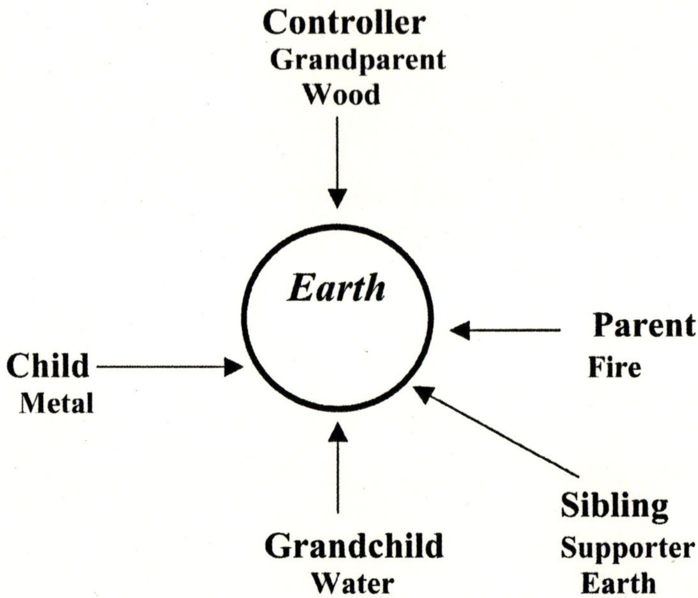
Controller
Grandparent
Wood
Earth
Parent
Fire
Child
Metal
Grandchild
Water
Sibling
Supporter
Earth

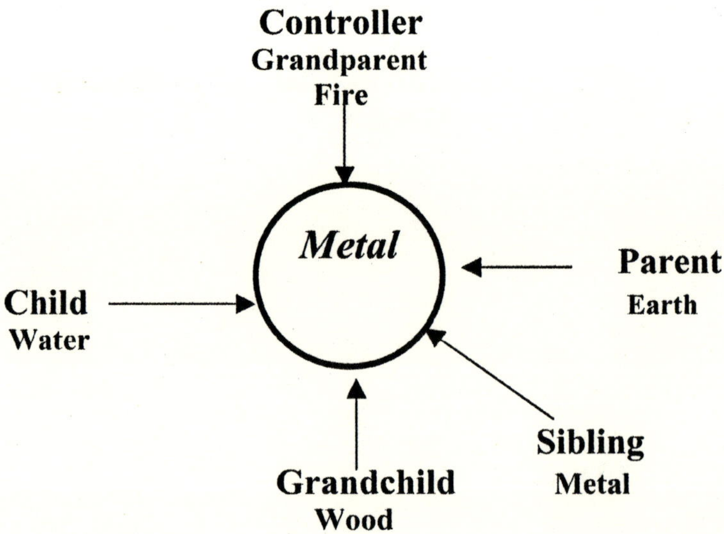
Controller
Grandparent
Fire
Metal
Parent
Earth
Child
Water
Grandchild
Wood
Sibling
Metal

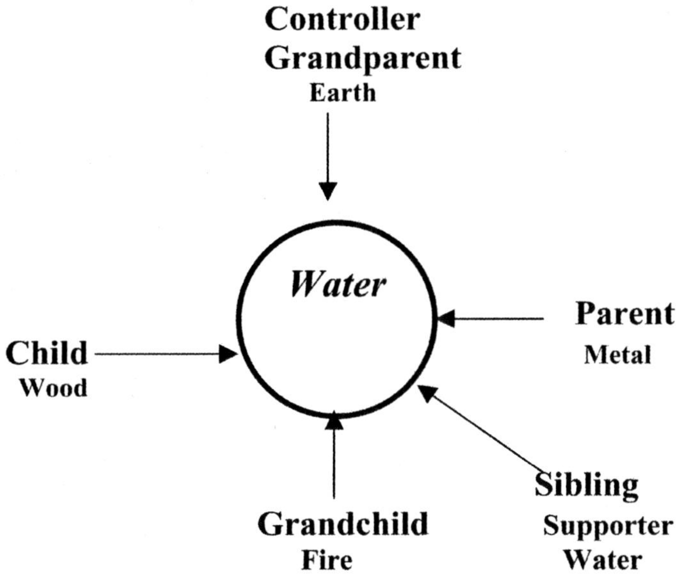
Controller
Grandparent
Earth
Water
Parent
Metal
Child
Wood
Sibling
Supporter
Water
Grandchild
Fire

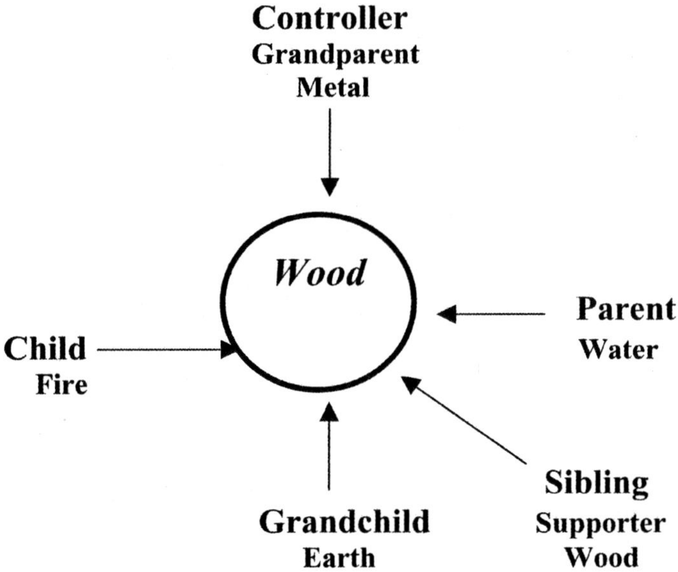
Controller
Grandparent
Metal
Wood
Parent
Water
Child
Fire
Sibling
Supporter
Wood
Grandchild
Earth

Table 3c

Element	Corrections for Excess	Corrections for Weakness
Water	Earth, Wood	Metal, Water
Wood	Metal, Fire	Water, Wood
Fire	Water, Earth	Wood, Fire
Earth	Wood, Metal	Fire, Earth
Metal	Fire, Water	Earth, Metal

The Five Elements interact in a variety of cycles, the major cycles are promotion, controlling and sedation cycles, they provide the basis for most applications of Asian arts. The following explains each cycle.

Promotion Cycle

The Promotion cycle is the Parent to Child relationship within the Five Elements. It is a cycle that nourishes, supplements or strengthens the child element, its influence can be favorable or unfavorable, depending on the condition of the elements. The following diagram illustrates the Promotion cycle.

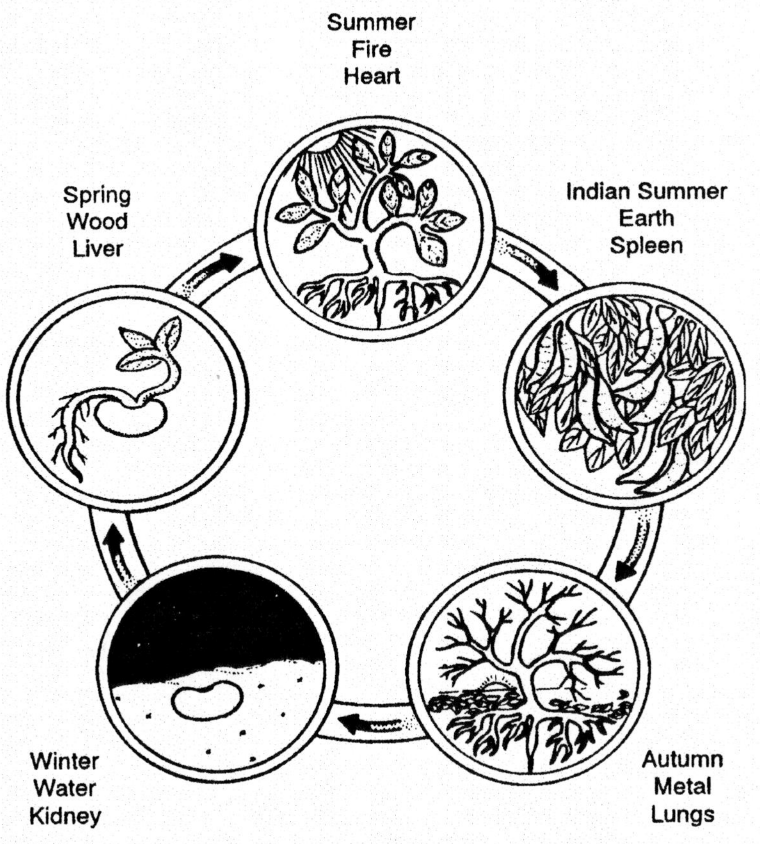

Promotion Cycle

1. If Water is placed on Wood, it will grow. Water is the mother of Wood.
2. If Wood is placed in a Fire, Fire will grow. Wood is the mother of Fire.
3. Fire will turn substances into Ashes or Earth. Fire is the Mother of Earth.
4. Metal is found within Earth. Earth is the Mother of Metal.
5. Metal can be liquefied into Water. Metal is the Mother of Water.

Controlling Cycle

The controlling cycle is the grandparent to grandchild relationship. Its influence can be favorable or unfavorable, depending on the conditions of the elements. The following diagram illustrates the controlling cycle.

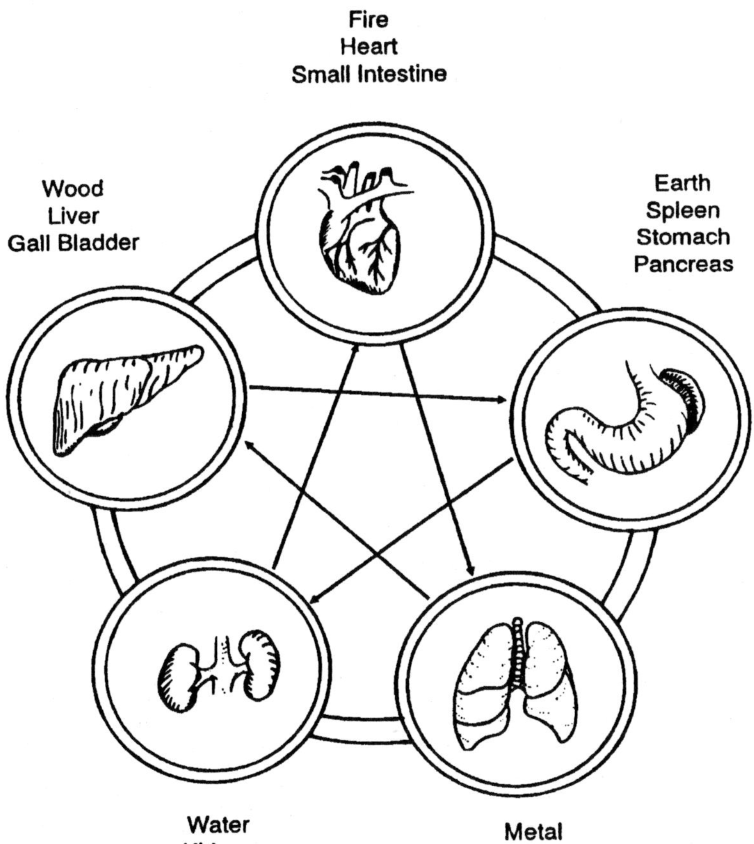

The arrows direct the controlling cycle sequence.

Controlling Cycle

1. Fire melts Metal or controls Metal. Grandparent relationship.
2. Metal cuts Wood or controls Wood. Grandparent relationship.
3. Wood absorbs nutrients from the Earth and controls Earth. Grandparent relationship.
4. Earth absorbs Water or controls Water. Grandparent relationship.
5. Water puts out Fire or controls Fire. Grandparent relationship.

Sedation Cycle

The Controlling cycle controls, dominates or weakens. When the controlling cycle is overactive and creates an imbalance, the Sedation cycle is used to correct the Controlling cycle. In most cases, the Controlling cycle creates unfavorable Health and needs to be corrected. Promotion and Sedation cycles are arranged identically, the only difference is the flow of energy, the Promotional cycle flows clockwise and the Sedation cycle flows counter-clockwise. All three cycles are used in Chinese Astrology, Feng Shui, Qi Gong and alchemy.

Sedation-Reduction Cycle

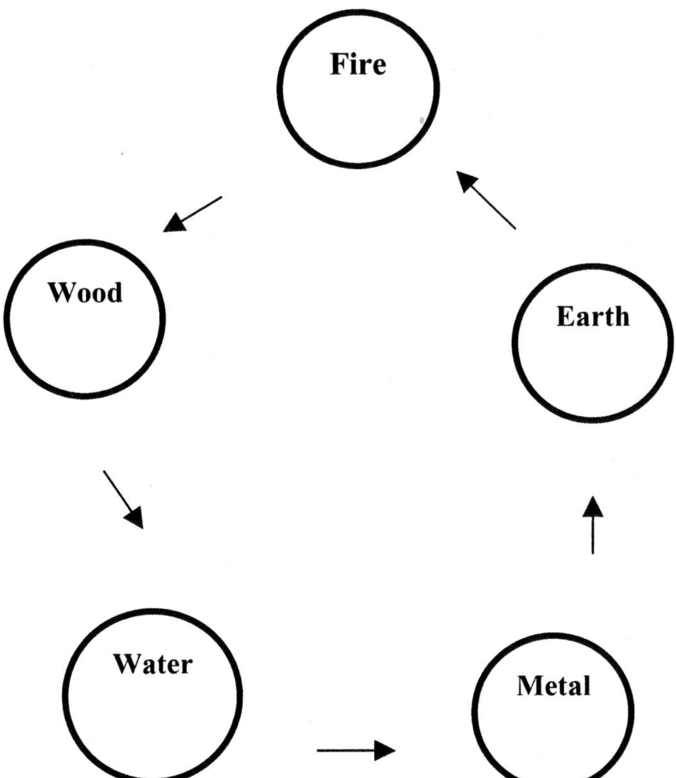

Sedation Cycle

1. Water is the child of Metal. Water takes from Metal, reducing its influence.
2. Metal is the child of Earth. Metal takes from Earth, reducing its influence.
3. Earth is the child of Fire. Earth takes from Fire, reducing its influence.
4. Fire is the child of Wood. Fire takes from Wood, reducing its influence.
5. Wood is the child of Water. Wood takes from Water, reducing its influence.

Five Element Correspondences

The following section includes general attributes for each of the Five Elements. This section is presented to offer a comprehensive view of the five elements.

Water

Water can nourish or deteriorate. Water people communicate well, are gentle, caring and susceptible to fear. They are not straightforward; they prefer a soft, gentle and indirect way of interaction. Water people are good at both sides of communication, listening and talking. They use their emotional sensitivity to influence people and can be greatly influenced by others and their environment. Water people unify others with emotional energy and understanding. They trust their intuition and use flexibility and perseverance to succeed.

Element	Water
Movement	Adaptable, Flexible
Season	Winter
Direction	North
Planet	Mercury
Color	Blue, Black
Compatible Profession	Teaching, communication, transportation, fishing, divination, lecturing, healers.
Relationships	Water is the sibling. Wood is the child. Fire is the grandchild. Earth is the grandparent. Metal is the parent.
Organs	Kidneys – Rat Urinary Bladder—Pig
Emotions	Gentleness Fear
Sense Orifice	Hearing
Tissues	Bones
Taste	Salty
Spirit	Zhi – Will Power

Wood

Wood represents growth. It is expansive and provides direction to achieving goals. Wood people can turn resources into products, ideas into profits, and believe expansion or growth will resolve any problems. Wood people are very sociable and are almost always surrounded by others; they have good verbal skills. Woods are extroverted and love to accomplish or complete activities.

Wood people can have strong tempers and feel frustrated when other people fail to perform to their standards. They can be scattered, spreading themselves and their resources too thin. Wood types may find it difficult to express their inner emotions, have few close friends and can suffer from feeling inadequate. They can handle great amounts of pressure. Wood types are practical people who are always looking to the future.

Element	Wood
Movement	Growth, Ascension.
Season	Spring
Direction	East
Planet	Jupiter
Color	Green
Compatible Profession	Education, writing, publishing, apparel manufacturing, fashion, herbal products, wood related industries.
Relationships	Water is parent. Wood is sibling. Fire is child. Earth is grandchild. Metal is grandparent.
Organs	Liver – Rabbit Gallbladder – Tiger
Sense	Vision
Taste	Sour
Tissues	Tendons
Emotions	Kindness Anger
Spirit	Hun – Direction, Planning

Fire

Fire warms, clarifies and comforts, but can also burn and destroy. It can illuminate or bring light to a situation, or can create explosive actions. Fire people are leaders, motivators and take-charge people. They are highly charismatic, very self-driven, and passionate. If nothing is going on, they will ignite a spark to create something. They are adventurous and are always looking for something new. Change is a predominant theme for them, and they often leap before looking. This can create great successes and great problems. Fire people want to be the center of attention.

Fire people are good speakers, but can be poor listeners. They are creators and think and act fast. They are brave, take on all challenges, and are good warriors. Fire people can be flamboyant, filled with passion, and make life exciting. They need to keep their excitement, passion and enthusiasm in balance and develop patience.

Element	Fire
Movement	Active, vitality.
Season	Summer
Direction	South
Planet	Mars
Color	Red
Compatible Profession	Restaurant, alcohol, electricity, entertainment, power sources.
Relationships	Wood is the parent. Fire is sibling. Earth is the child. Metal is the grandchild. Water is the grandparent.
Organs	Heart—Horse Small Intestine – Snake
Sense	Taste
Taste	Bitter
Tissues	Blood Vessels
Emotions	Joy, Love Hastiness, Impatience, Hatred
Spirit	Shen: 1. Spirit of the Heart 2. Collective Spirit of all Organs

Earth

Earth provides stability and is a transformer. In the Five Elements, it is the transforming energy from one season to another or from one element to another. Fairness is often a predominant quality in an Earth person and they tend to be chronic worriers, in fact they may worry about everything, not only their direct life, but everything in the universe. They are steady and do not move as fast as others, but what they lack in speed, they make up with consistency and longevity. They do not like to waste their time in grand schemes or ideas; instead, they plow through the realities of a situation.

Earth people make wonderful managers or organizers; they can be trusted with implementing a plan. However, their focus, practicality and perseverance may result in a single-mindedness, which hinders versatility and the ability to handle multiple factors simultaneously. Earth people are not overly emotional, but are sensitive. They resolve emotional problems in practical, concrete ways. Earth people expect the rest of the world to view life as they do, if they do not, Earth types can become stubborn and rigid. They respond well to change, if the change is slow and gradual, abrupt changes disturb them.

Element	Earth
Movement	Stability, stillness.
Season	Indian Summer.
Direction	North East, South West, Center
Planet	Saturn
Color	Yellow, beige.
Compatible Profession	Construction, real estate, attorney, judges, human resources, management, consultation.
Relationships	Fire is the parent. Earth is the sibling. Metal is the child. Water is the grandchild. Wood is the grandparent.
Tissues	Flesh
Organs	Spleen – Ox, Sheep Stomach – Dragon, Dog
Emotions	Openness, Fairness Worry
Spirit	Yi – Concentration

Metal

Metal can be a precious substance, for example, Gold, or a destructive device, a sword. Metal communicates information; it can relay information smoothly. Metal people can gather others for positive goals or negative objectives. They can be focused, emotional, intuitive, confident and aggressive in pursuing goals. Metals tend to be loners, isolated and often withdraw. Metal types may be stubborn, driven by an inner faith whether they are right or wrong. They can be extremely driven to pursue their goals. When problems arise, they will turn inward to find answers, and cannot be expected to communicate their inner feelings. Metals can be successful in any profession, and can also motivate others to achieve common objectives.

Metals can be susceptible to sadness, which can dominate their life. If they become more flexible and open, they will develop loyal friendships. Metal represents righteousness, justice and truth, as well as sadness, grief, and longing.

Element	Metal
Movement	Inward
Season	Fall
Direction	West, North West
Planet	Venus
Color	White, Gold
Compatible Profession	Metal related industries, strategic management, automobile industry and jewelry.
Relationships	Water is the child. Wood is the grandchild. Fire is the grandparent. Earth is the parent. Metal is the sibling.
Tissues	Flesh
Organ	Lungs – Cock Large Intestine – Monkey
Emotions	Courage Sadness, Depression
Spirit	Po – Corporeal Soul

Chapter 4

Beginning Qi Gong

Five Element Organ Rejuvenation

Originating from the Mysterious Mother,
five element organ rejuvenation harmonizes internal organs,
magically producing joy and love in daily life.
The Mysterious Mother is the source of Spiritual Qi Gong,
know the offspring but stay with the Mysterious Mother,
balance and health are assured.

In most systems of self-development harmonizing emotions is a primary goal; it is the foundation for health and vitality. Qi Gong practices are particularly effective in balancing stress and negative emotions. Each organ has a positive and negative set of emotions that influence organ function; stress and unfavorable emotions drain energy and contribute to many diseases. Figure 4a illustrates each organ and their corresponding negative emotions. Five Element Organ Rejuvenation are the foundation Qi Gong practices in Spiritual Qi Gong, they can be practiced for a few minutes or up to an hour. It is helpful to have an anatomy book available if you are not familiar with the internal organs.

When practicing each Qi Gong meditation, spend as much time as necessary during each stage until you experience the described feeling, sensation or process. Spend from weeks to a year at any stage; the benefits will be achieved only when you have mastered each step. Each person is unique and there is no set duration of time to practice that fits all people, your daily experience determines your level of cultivation. The fruit of these practices appear through consistent, dedicated practice. Theoretical mastery has no true benefit without actually experiencing these meditations. Practice leads to direct experience and achievement; theory is secondary and does not provide direct experience of one's true nature.

Figure 4a

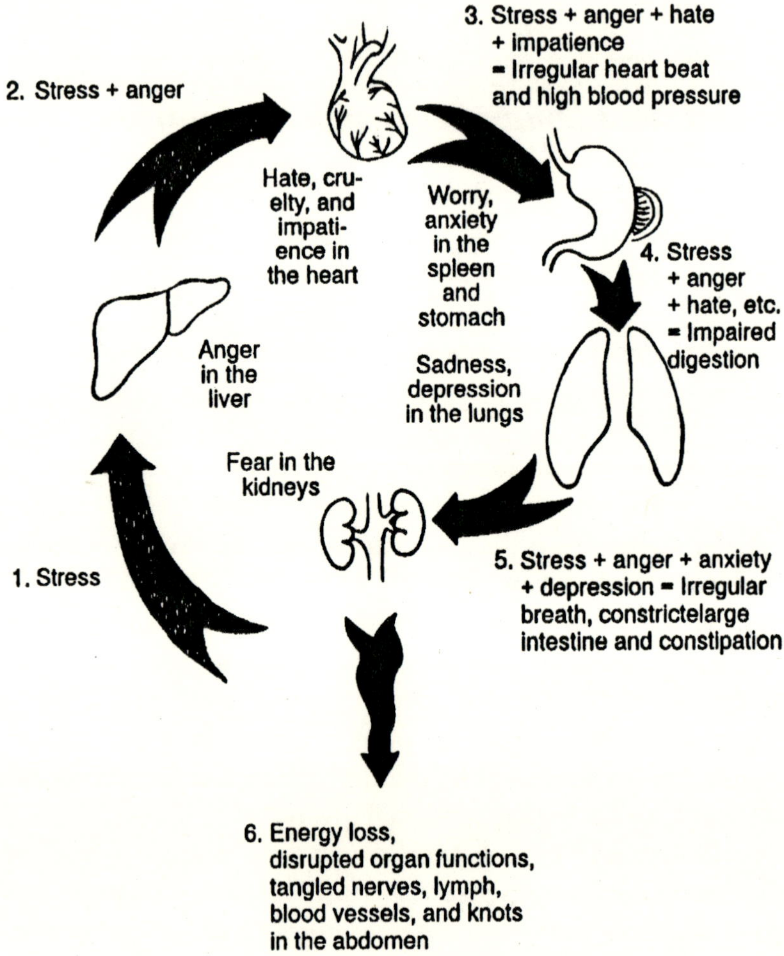
3. Stress + anger + hate
+ impatience
= Irregular heart beat
and high blood pressure
2. Stress + anger
Hate, cru-
elty, and
impati-
ence in
the heart
Worry,
anxiety
in the
spleen
and
stomach
4. Stress
+ anger
+ hate, etc.
= Impaired
digestion
Anger
in the
liver
Sadness,
depression
in the lungs
Fear in the
kidneys
1. Stress
5. Stress + anger + anxiety
+ depression = Irregular
breath, constrictelarge
intestine and constipation
6. Energy loss,
disrupted organ functions,
tangled nerves, lymph,
blood vessels, and knots
in the abdomen

Table 4a lists major Five Elements Organ Rejuvenation for Qi Gong, specifically that Harmonize emotions and reduce stress.

Table 4a

Element	Organ	Color	Sound	Positive Emotions	Negative Emotions
Water	Kidney Bladder	Blue Black	Woooo Like blowing out a candle	Gentleness	Fear
Wood	Liver Gallbladder	Green	Shhhh Like Shhhhhhing a little child	Kindness	Anger
Fire	Heart Small Intestine	Red	Haw	Joy, Love	Hastiness Hate
Earth	Spleen Stomach	Yellow	Whooo The sound comes from the throat.	Openness	Worry
Metal	Lung Large Intestine	White	SSSSS	Courage	Sadness Depression
	San Jiao	None	Heeeee	None	Balances all areas

The Five Element Organ Rejuvenation
Figure 4a

1. Begin by sitting naturally in a chair, open your eyes and place your mind's attention in the Lungs, take a slow, full inhale, breathing into the abdomen.
2. Think of sadness and depression, take one long exhale while making the SSSSSSSSSSSSSSS sound and release sadness and depression during the exhale.
3. Once you complete the exhale, close your eyes, place your hands face up on your thighs, smile while focusing your mind's attention in the white Lungs and repeat courage to yourself. Do this for 30-60 seconds.
4. Repeat steps 1-3 three times.
5. Open your eyes and place your mind's attention in the Kidneys, take a full inhale.
6. Think of fear and take one long exhale while making the Wooooo sound, release fear during the exhale.
7. Once you complete the exhale, close your eyes, place your hands face up on your thighs, smile while focusing your mind's eye into the blue-black Kidneys and repeat gentleness to yourself. Do this for 30-60 seconds.
8. Repeat steps 5-7 three times.
9. Repeat this procedure for the Liver, Heart and Spleen. Do the sounds in the following order, which is the promotion or creation cycle, Lungs, Kidneys, Liver, Heart, Spleen and San Jiao.

Figure 4a
Five Element Organ Rejuvenation: Healing Sounds

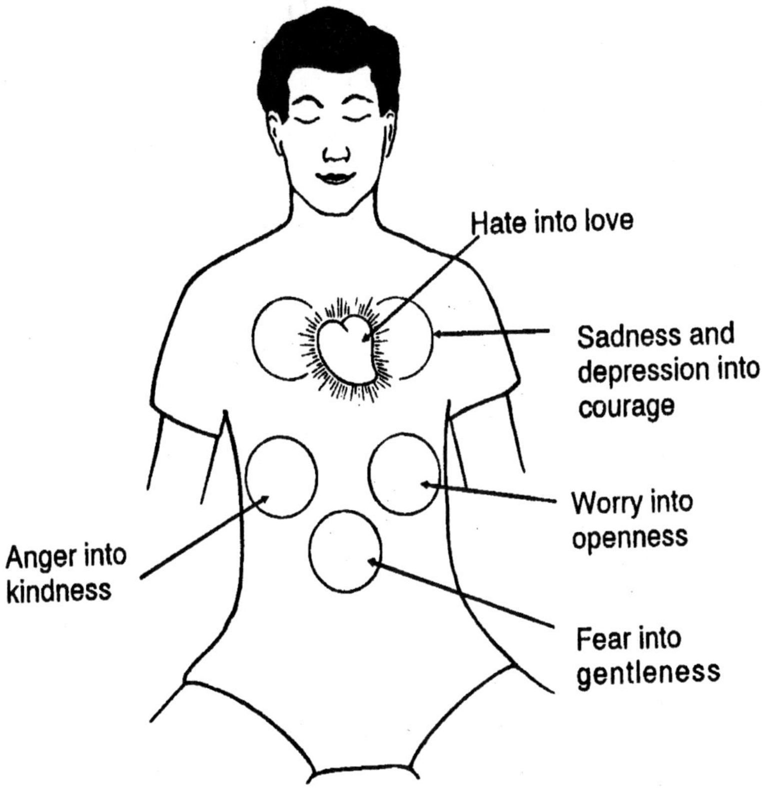

Five Element Organ Rejuvenation: Smiling Qi Gong See Figure 4b

1. Begin by sitting in a chair or on the floor, your spine should be straight and place the tip of your tongue to your palate or roof of the mouth. Hold your hands in your lap, folding them together.
2. Smile and place you mind's attention in the red Heart and repeat the words Joy and Love; feel Joy and Love in the Heart. Do this for one to three minutes.
3. Move your attention into the white Lungs, smile and repeat the word courage, feel courage in the Lungs. Do this for one to three minutes.
4. Move your attention to the green Liver, smile and repeat the word kindness, feel kindness in the Liver. Do this for one to three minutes.
5. Move your attention to the yellow Spleen, smile and repeat the word openness, feel openness in the Spleen. Do this for one to three minutes.
6. Move your attention to the blue-black Kidneys, smile and repeat the word gentleness, feel gentleness in the Kidneys. Do this for one to three minutes.
7. Move your attention behind the navel, focus there for three to five minutes.

   Gently open your eyes, stretch and enjoy.

Develop a daily routine of practice, in general do all Five Element Sounds and complete the Five Element Smile, this will harmonize all organs. If an organ is out of balance spend more time with that organ, if an organ is in excess or overactive, perform the *sound* for that organ 6-12 times. If an organ is deficient or weak, spend more time on that organ during the Five Element Smile.

Figure 4b
The Five Element Organ Rejuvenation: Smile Qi Gong

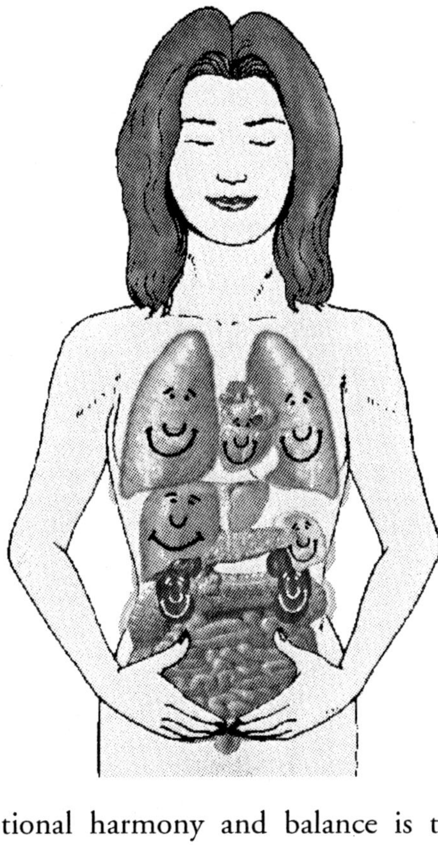

Achieving emotional harmony and balance is the initial aspect of Spiritual Qi Gong and the refinement of a person; the ups and downs of life are often great motivators, but when that lifestyle is the normal everyday way of living, growth and transformation does not occur. Transformation implies a change in the way one lives life, the foundation cultivation practices, Five Element Sounds and Smile calm, relax and harmonize emotions.

Chapter 5

Heavenly Orbit Qi Gong

Guided by the subtle realm,
heavenly stars and planets circulate in natural rhythm.
Spiritual Qi Gong follows this heavenly rhythm,
circulating cosmic forces within generates vitality and longevity.

The beauty of the solar system, its planets and stars floating throughout space in endless cycles is a magnificent example of the Universe's maco cycle. Oriental Medicine views each person as a microcosm of the Universe, cycles which flow throughout the Universe also flow within each person. Each person is comprised of energy or Qi and has energy pathways, channels or meridians flowing from limb to limb; connecting every tendon, muscle, organ and cell throughout the body. There are many types of meridians or pathways, two major ones are the major Yang (Du) and Yin (Ren) channels or pathways. The Yang-Du channel emerges at the perineum (about one inch about the anus), connects to the bottom of the spine, rises up the spine into the brain, then turns down into the palate. The major Yin-Ren begins at the perineum, moves up to the palate where it meets with the Yang-Du Channel. These two channels are really one channel, one orbit or circuit (Figure 5a). Energy or Qi flows or circulates through this orbit in the same way planets circulate through space. This orbit has many names, for example, Heavenly Orbit, Orbit, Microcosmic Orbit or Dharma Wheel.

Qi or energy naturally flows throughout the body and channels, when stress, pressure or trauma occurs, whether emotional or physical, a blockage of this energy occurs. This blockage causes physical or emotional stagnation, resulting in discomfort or pain, most importantly, Qi is not circulating properly, failing to nourish and energize the body. This lack of nourishment can lead to chronic illness and depression of the immune system, when Qi flows normally all of the body is nourished and energized. The two major channels, Ren and Du, control and manage other channels in the body. They are functionally similar to reservoirs, gathering, storing and distributing energy to other channels, internal organs, glands, lymphatic, nervous and skeletal systems. The Heavenly Orbit meditation enhances energy flow through these two major channels and recycles energy, preventing loss of life force and increases vitality. The Heavenly Orbit is the foundation for all Qi Gong practices and the basis of Spiritual Qi Gong. There are many ways to practice the Orbit meditation; in my experience the following techniques are efficient and effective.

The Tan Tien

Tan Tien means energy field or area. In Taoist energy cultivation there are four major Tan Tiens: Navel Tan Tien, Solar Plexus Tan Tien, Heart Tan Tien and Third Eye Tan Tien. The navel tan tien is the most common known in Qi Gong, it is a meeting location of the Eight Extra Ordinary channels, a matrix of acupuncture pathways that can gather, store and distribute energy, it is the primary location for Spiritual Qi Gong and alchemy. Each tan tien is a passageway into the subtle realm, it can be considered an area of void or empty space, and within this empty space the Universe may be revealed. A basic procedure is to blend or mix energies in the Tan Tien, which transforms and refines them. This refined energy is circulated throughout the body energizing and vitalizing it. Tan Tiens are a spiritual womb. This womb is where conscious awareness of the immortal body is formed, nourished and grown, leading to direct experience of one's true nature.

Heavenly Orbit Qi Gong

Part 1

1. Sit in a chair or on the floor cross-legged or in the lotus position, your back should be straight and fold your hands together. One way to fold your hands is like clapping your hands, holding them in your lap. Place the tip of your tongue to the palate-roof of the mouth, in a comfortable position. The most important thing is to relax and feel comfortable.
2. Place your mind's attention (Yi) in the perineum; it is located two inches above the anus, gently inhale from the perineum up the spine to the top of the head, while inhaling count one, exhale from the top of the head down to the perineum, while counting two. Inhale from the perineum to the top of the head counting three and exhale down to the perineum counting four. Repeat this process until you reach the count of ten. The breathing is natural and comfortable.

   Breathing up and down the Orbit guides energy through the acupuncture channels, causing it to circulate smoothly, clearing blockages or points of stagnation. Common sensations are tingling, pulsating, vibrating or electric feelings throughout the body; these are all favorable sensations and as the channels become clearer and more open, the energy circulation and accumulation becomes increasingly favorable and enjoyable. Figure 5a illustrates the flow of the Orbit.

Figure 5a

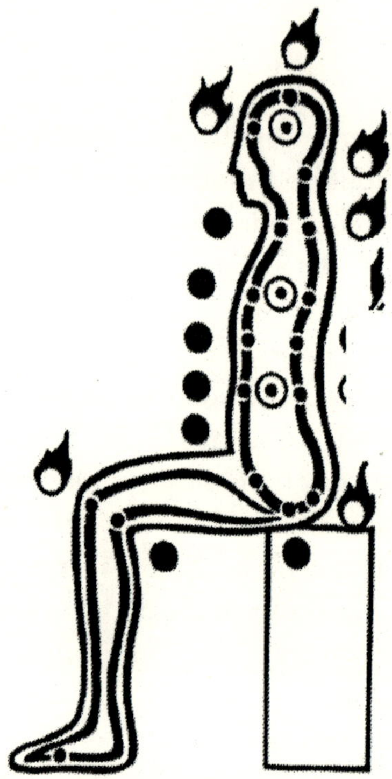

This meditation should be practiced for 20-30 minutes. It can be practiced longer or shorter depending on your schedule, be flexible and relaxed about the process and amount of time practiced. Create a realistic plan that meets your individual needs.

When you are ready to stop, place one hand over your navel, palm facing the navel and the other over the first. Concentrate your mind's attention behind your navel, about an inch or two, and circulate your mind's attention around the inside of the navel, like a small circle; spiraling can be horizontal or vertical. Do this 18-36 times clockwise, then 18-36 times counter-clockwise. The spiraling gathers energy and stores it in the area behind the navel; this area is referred to as the Tan Tien, which means energy field. It is like a battery for the body, it safely stores energy.

If energy is not stored in the Tan Tien, it may be stored in areas or Acupuncture points that could cause physical or emotional stress, it is vital to always complete each Qi Gong meditation by storing Qi in the navel.

Part 2

1. When you feel comfortable with part one begin in the same way but this time circulate energy through the orbit without counting. Begin in the perineum and move your mind's attention up the spine to the top of the head, then down the front of the body to the perineum, continue moving up and down until you feel the energy inside your body.
2. Finish by storing energy in the Tan Tien, behind the navel.

Part 3

1. Take your normal sitting position, place the tip of your tongue to the palate and concentrate your attention about 1-½ inches below and behind the navel. Concentrate until you feel energy, tingling or an electric sensation in this region, when it occurs move your mind's attention to the perineum, up the spine to the crown or top of the head and down the palate, throat, chest, solar plexuses and perineum. Continue this circulation while breathing naturally and until you feel energy throughout your body. Do this for 10-20 minutes, then collect and store the energy in the Tan Tien, behind the navel.

Part 4

In this section we gather, circulate and store external energies into the body and Tan Tien; they include Heavenly, Cosmic and Earthly forces, figure 5b.

1. Begin after completing part 3, place your mind in the Earth, deep below your feet and feel its energy, see and feel it connect to the Tan Tien. The energy beams or is directed into the Tan Tien.

2. Place your mind's attention in the solar system-Heavenly energy, visualize and feel its energy beam into the crown (top of the head), down the Ren channel and into the Tan Tien; this energy continually beams into the Tan Tien.
3. Place your mind's attention in front of your third eye or between your eyebrows, this area relates to the Cosmic Forces of plants, oceans, lakes, mountains and planetary life; visualize and feel this energy beam into your third eye and down into the Tan Tien.
4. There are three forces being drawn into the Tan Tien, split your consciousness into four parts, be aware of all three forces collecting in the Tan Tien. Spiral your mind's attention in the Tan Tien facilitating the collection of the three forces. Once you feel energy build in the Tan Tien, circulate it by moving your attention through the Orbit for 5-20 minutes, finish by collecting energy in the Tan Tien.

Diagram 5b

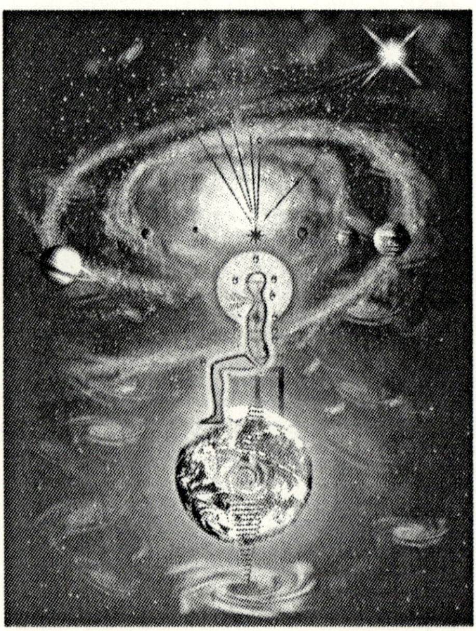

Chapter 6

Five Elements and Five Shen

The creator, Tao or God is the root of life and can be found in every branch of life. The five elements are one way to view life and are an integral aspect of Spiritual Qi Gong. The five elements contain root and branch within its principle application; each element corresponds to a geographical direction, planet, internal organ, emotion and sensory organ. These relationships are used to refine, unify and realize the integration of the root of life within human form. From a macro view, human life consists of heavenly and earthly energies: the essences of stars, planets, water, mountains, lakes, trees, plants, etc. They are branches of the subtle realm; Qi provides life to these branches. These dynamic Universal energies create human form, Spiritual Qi Gong traces human consciousness and spirit through these branches to realize its original nature.

The Universe is a living being, every aspect of it has a type of living Qi. Qi is the Universe and the Universe is full of Qi. From a micro perspective, every aspect of human form is Qi; bones, muscles, organs, glands and blood are Qi. In Oriental Medicine each internal organ contributes towards creating vital substances: Qi, Blood and Body Fluids, they promote health and vitality. These organs relate to and are influenced by the five elements and their correspondences, especially direction and planets. The subtle realm creates the five directions: East-Wood-Jupiter-Liver, South-Fire-Mars-Heart, West-Metal-Venus-Lungs and Center-Earth-Saturn-Spleen. Science has shown atoms of stars and planets are the same found in the human body. The directions are beacons of energy and contribute towards the creation of human life and spirit. Planets are branches of the subtle realm; in Spiritual Qi Gong they reunite, nourish and guide a person to realize their true spiritual nature.

The five elements are more accurately referred to as the five phases, they make up one phase or process, each element or phase can not be separated or extracted, they work together as one unit. This process is a fundamental principle of Spiritual Qi Gong, all phases-elements, internal organs, directions and planets are one unified whole, never separated. Beginning with conscious awareness of this reality the foundation is set for Spiritual Qi Gong. This process begins by turning one's attention into the internal organs, experiencing the virtues, directional energies and corresponding spirit contained in the organs. With practice each person will transcend their physical and emotional bodies and unite with Universal life; the oneness of life is experienced.

Human life has three major aspects: Spiritual, Mental and Physical, harmony among these three is the key principle in maintaining a healthy life. When mental or physical aspects become predominant, harmony and unity are dissipated, leading to a sense of isolation or separation from the whole. The longer and deeper this "false separation" develops, habits and patterns become intensified, producing a potent veil, blocking an awareness of one's true nature. Spiritual Qi Gong slowly and gently generates unity and harmony allowing one to directly experience their true nature.

The subtle realm is the root and the three aspects of life: Spiritual, Mental and Physical are branches, unifying these three branches allows a person to perceive they are also root. The human body consists of many branches, five major relationships include Kidneys, Lungs, Liver, Heart and Spleen; each of these internal organs corresponds to a five element and geographical energy. Unifying these branches, organs, elements and directions is the primary objective of Spiritual Qi Gong. This process is Taoist Alchemy. Unifying these aspects reveals a person's eternal, spiritual nature and facilitates its evolution. This is the ancient, esoteric process of realizing spiritual immortality.

Ancient Taoists viewed all of life as energy and referred to powerful life forces as spirits. The planets Jupiter, Mars, Venus, Mercury and Saturn and their related directions East, South, West, North and Center were considered potent life forces or spirits, because internal organs correspond to planets and their related directions, they were also referred to as spirits. Planetary spirit is internal organ spirit and internal organ spirit is human spirit. Spiritual Qi Gong develops conscious awareness of the undivided connection between these five spirits or aspects of life, allowing a profound experience of one's true, immortal nature. This is the first fruit of Spiritual Qi Gong cultivation.

In Oriental Medicine and Taoist practice there are two aspects to Shen or Spirit, the first consists of the "small five shen" located in the organs, the second is the "big shen" which resides in the Heart, this "big" shen is the composite of the five shen in the organs. Unifying the five shen is the essence of Spiritual Qi Gong; this unification is a "birthing" process that reveals one's immortal, spiritual body. The goal of Spiritual Qi Gong is to harmonize and integrate these "Spirits" or energies into one Shen, nourish this Shen with Universal Forces, expanding human consciousness and its capacity to absorb, digest and utilize higher levels of energy, preparing for complete union with the source of life, subtle realm, Tao, creator or God.

The following section explains each organ and its related spiritual aspect and alchemical associations. Table 6a and Figure 6a summarize these relationships; Figure 6b illustrates the unification process.

1. The physical aspect of life or Po spirit corresponds to the Lungs, planet Venus, nose and sense of smell; it has a strong attachment to the physical or material world.
2. The ethereal aspect of the spirit or Hun spirit corresponds to the Liver, Jupiter, eyes, sight, and direction or planning life; it is attached to subtle energy and spirit world.
3. "I" which is pronounced "EE", corresponds to focus, memory, concentration or the intention aspect of a person. "I" relates to the Spleen, Saturn, mouth and taste. It reflects the center and transformation functions.

4. Zhi spirit corresponds to will power, Kidneys, Mercury, ears and hearing. It reflects the genetic blueprint of life; with diligent cultivation the deepest aspects of our spiritual blueprint is revealed.
5. Shen, which means spirit, relates to the "Big" or "Small" spirit, in this case the application is the small spirit and corresponds to the Heart, Mars, tongue and speech.
6. The "Big" Shen is the collective, integrated spirit of all Shen.

Table 6a

The following chart summarizes the five elements.

Element	Spirit	Organ	Planet	Color	Sense Organ	Emotions	Quality
Water	Zhi Will Power	Kidneys	Mercury	Blue, Black	Ears, Hearing	Gentleness Fear	Cold
Wood	Hun Ethereal	Liver	Jupiter	Green	Eyes, Sight	Kindness Anger	Warm
Fire	Shen Spirit	Heart	Mars	Red	Tongue, Speech	Joy, Love Hate, Impatience	Hot
Earth	I Focus	Spleen	Saturn	Yellow	Mouth, Taste	Openness Worry	Neutral
Metal	Po Corporeal	Lungs	Venus	White	Lungs, Smell	Courageous Sadness	Cool

Figure 6a

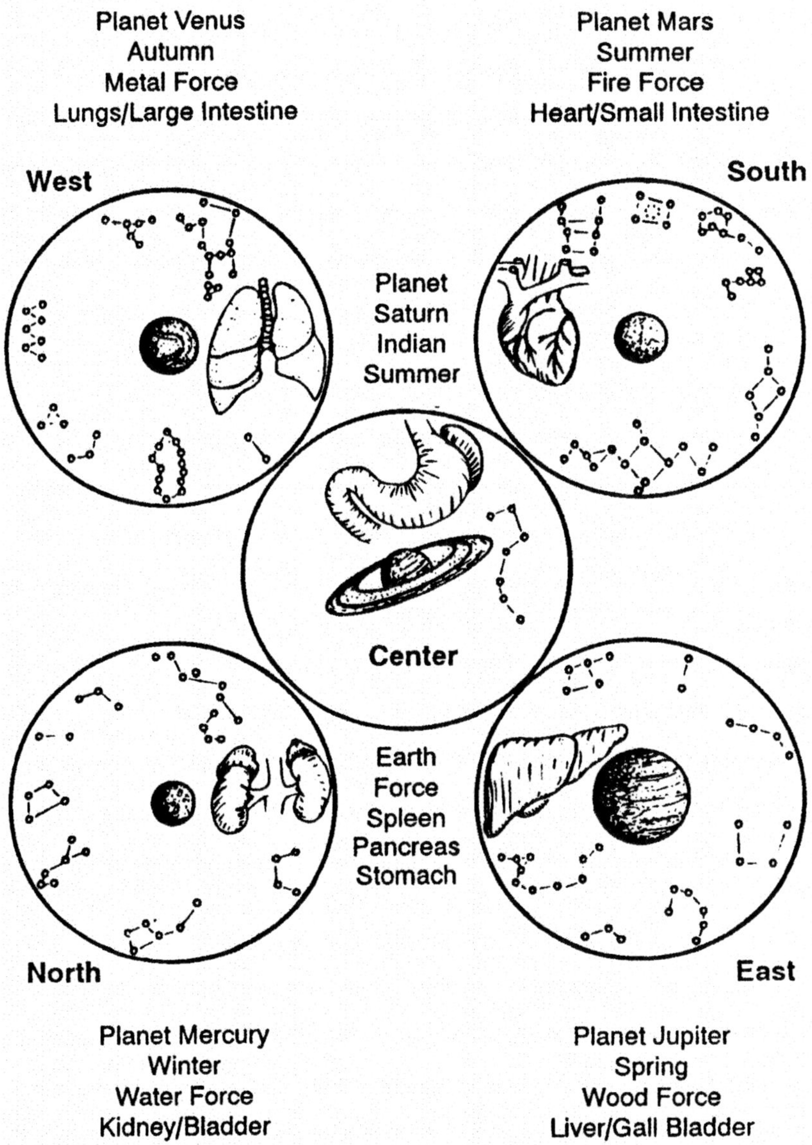
Planet Venus
Autumn
Metal Force
Lungs/Large Intestine
Planet Mars
Summer
Fire Force
Heart/Small Intestine
West
South
Planet
Saturn
Indian
Summer
Center
Earth
Force
Spleen
Pancreas
Stomach
North
East
Planet Mercury
Winter
Water Force
Kidney/Bladder
Planet Jupiter
Spring
Wood Force
Liver/Gall Bladder

Figure 6b

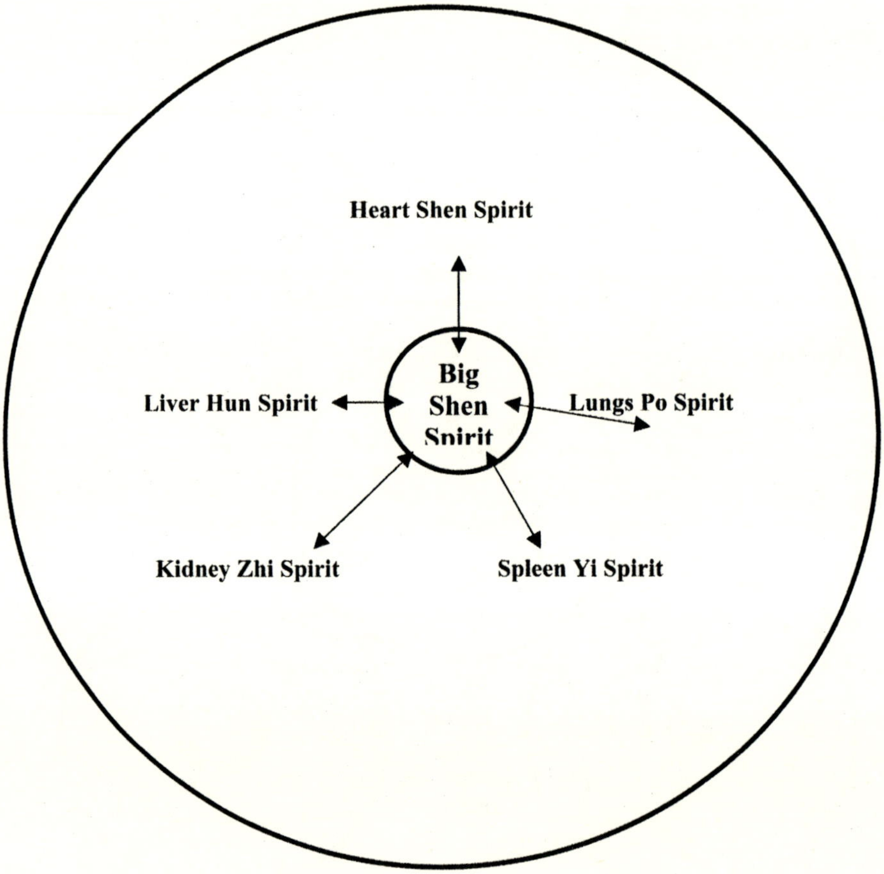
Heart Shen Spirit
Big
Shen
Spirit
Liver Hun Spirit
Lungs Po Spirit
Kidney Zhi Spirit
Spleen Yi Spirit

Chapter 7

Eight Treasures Qi Gong

Cultivating the Eight Extraordinary-Psychic Channels

Self-generation and transformation are expressions of the subtle realm.
Unite the Five Elements and form the immortal pearl,
this is the foundation for experiencing the eternal nature of life.

Stars, planets and human life exist within a Universal energy web, paralleling this Universal structure is a human web comprised of acupuncture channels or pathways. These networks of energy channels contain eight special pathways; they are the eight extraordinary or psychic channels. These are the first channels developed in the body and function at the deepest and most constitutional level; they have a special relationship with the three treasures: Jing, Qi and Shen, the energetic DNA of human life. In a similar way an astrological birth chart reveals a constitutional condition, the Eight Extraordinary channels reveal this condition as well. These special channels reflect the Karmic or constitutional blueprint of life. Table 7 summarizes applicable Qi Gong information for each of the Eight Extraordinary channels. While practicing Qi Gong meditations, one goal is to harmonize these Eight Extraordinary channels and their current conditions. From an Alchemical perspective, transformation must occur in these channels for a person to change.

In the same way the Sun and Moon are physical entities with enormous energy, each internal organ contains an enormous amount of life force. In Taoist alchemy, the Sun and Moon, as well as internal organs obtain their energy from another source, the subtle realm. Each organ provides functions that maintain life; this is common knowledge in the western community, what is not common is each organ is the residence of emotions and virtues. When they are unbalanced they influence functions of organs, potentially altering their performance and diminishing their functioning and health. Additionally, if an organ is diseased it may contribute to imbalances of related emotions. The following meditations transform negative or unfavorable energy-emotions into positive or favorable energy. Transforming emotions is a major step in the refinement process, it is necessary to clear and harmonize the eight psychic channels for transformation at the deepest levels. The refinement process allows a person to gather and digest greater amounts of subtle energies, for example, when gathering Heavenly, Cosmic and Earthy forces, our capacity to digest and utilize this energy depends on the level of refinement. As we refine energy, our body and its organs, glands, nerves, energy and channels transform. There are three major benefits:

The first is transforming unfavorable emotions into favorable and usable energy; this practice has a profound emotional influence.

The second benefit is the formation of the pearl, the crystallization of the body-mind-spirit essences.

The third benefit is clearing and vitalizing the eight extraordinary channels and transcending the physical and emotional bodies. When practicing this Qi Gong it is common to feel happier, stronger and inspired about life. There may be euphoric sensations throughout the body as refined energy is circulated throughout these eight extraordinary channels. The following explains these Qi Gong meditations.

Table 7
Eight Extraordinary Channels

Channel	Qualities
Chong Mai Center Channel	Relates to destiny, the blueprint of life and how we relate to ourselves.
Ren Mai Front Channel	Relates to bonding with the world, our connection to life and how we relate to our resources obtained in life, whether love from parents, intimate relationships or love of self.
Du Mai Back Channel	Relates to independence, movement and separation from parents or dependencies. The ability to make these changes in a health way.
Dai Mai Belt Channel	Relates to holding or retaining. When any issues of these eight channels are not resolved they can be retained in this channel. Positive attributes also are retained here.
Yin Qiao Interior Leg Channel	Relates to how we stand up to ourselves, seeing our role in life with Clarity and obtaining an understanding of the meaning and purpose of life. It is how well we can feel comfortable in our position in life. Dealing with what is, not so much with what may occur.
Yang Qiao Lateral LegChannel	Relates to how we stand up to the world, how we present ourselves to the world. It also reflects how we view the world and how we feel we need to project ourselves into this world. Issues creating difficulties from relating to the external world can manifest from these channels.
Yin Wei Mai Inner Arm Channel	Relates to how one deals with stages of life: aging, relationships, race, gender, profession; relating to the past and future and how one feels about their place and role in life. Its focus is on position or space in life.
Yang Wei Lateral Arm Channel	Relates to how one responds to day-to-day activities and dealing with time issues, e.g. death, achievement levels in giving time frames, etc.

Eight Treasures Cultivation

This meditation expands on the Heavenly Orbit Qi Gong, there are many variations to this practice, the one presented is the most direct in my experience.

Part 1

1. Begin after the Orbit meditation, visualize a cauldron (figure 7a) behind the navel or in the lower Tan Tien. This cauldron is a place to recycle, refine and transform energy and is used throughout the remainder of this cultivation or alchemy.
2. Place your attention in the Kidneys and be aware of any fear and cold, fear and cold manifest in the Kidneys, focus on this until the energy-emotion is strong, at this time move the energy into the cauldron; spiral this energy and condense it until it takes the form of a small crystal or pearl.
3. Place your attention in the Heart and allow hastiness, impatience, hatred and heat to appear; after you feel this energy move it into the cauldron, mix or couple this energy with the existing energy in the cauldron. Spiral these energies forming the pearl. The cauldron is a transformer and changes energies into a neutral or original force.
4. Place your attention in the Liver and allow any anger, warmth or dryness to manifest. Upon feeling this energy, emotion and temperature in the Liver, move it into the cauldron, mix and blend it with the existing energy.
5. Place your attention in the Lungs and allow any sadness, depression, coolness and wetness to manifest. Upon feeling the qualities of the Lungs, move it into the cauldron and blend it with the existing energy.
6. Place your attention in the Spleen, be aware of any worry and allow it to manifest. When you feel this energy move it into the

cauldron and mix it with the existing energy. Spiral and collect all the energy nourishing the pearl.

7. When spiraling energy at each stage, spiral and circle the energy in clockwise or counter-clockwise directions, focus on gathering the energy into a small pearl or ball, this pearl is the essence of the internal organs, its refined energy and related spirit; it is the foundation of alchemy.

Figure 7a

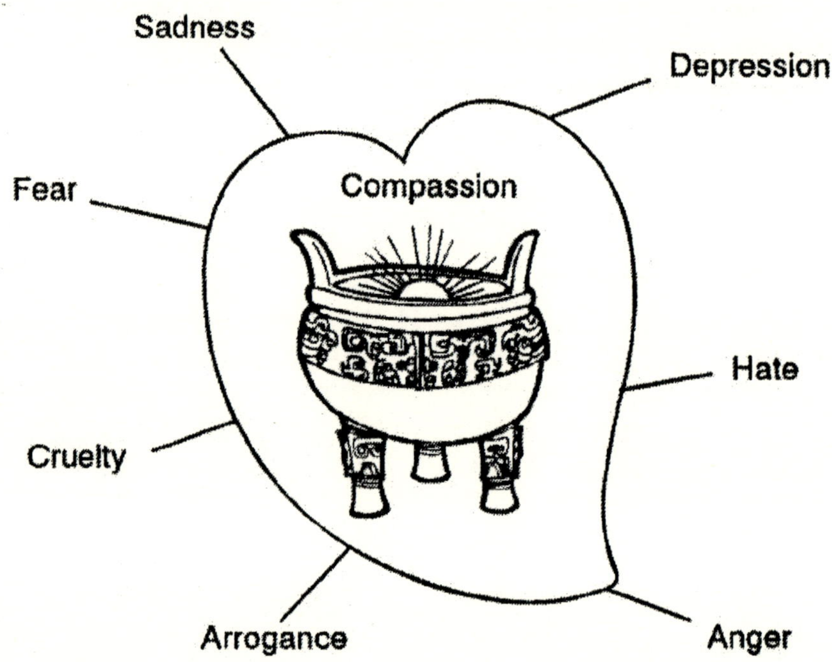

Part 2

1. Place your mind's attention in the cauldron, feel the pearl or energy ball and move it down to the perineum, then into the Du channel, up the spine into the crown, down the palate and through the Ren channel. Circulate this pearl through the Orbit

for a few minutes. Finish by moving the pearl into the cauldron and collect it.

2. Move the pearl into the Kidneys and see the pearl and Kidneys become a blue color and full of gentleness. See and feel this for a few minutes.
3. Move the pearl from the Kidneys to the Liver, see and feel the pearl and Liver become green and full of kindness. See and feel this for a few minutes.
4. Move the pearl from the Liver to the Heart, see the pearl and Heart become red and full of love. See and feel this for a few minutes.
5. Move the pearl from the Heart to the Spleen, see and feel the pearl and Spleen become yellow and full of openness. See and feel this for a few minutes.
6. Move the pearl from the Spleen to the Lungs, see the pearl and Lungs become white and full of courage. See and feel this for a few minutes.
7. Repeat this flow and sequence three to nine cycles or more.
8. Finish by bringing the pearl into the cauldron, spiral and collect it.

Part 3

1. Feel the pearl in the cauldron; guide it through the Orbit 18-36 times.
2. Bring the pearl to the perineum and move it into the thrusting channel. This channel is in the middle of body and runs from the perineum to the crown. Begin by circulating the pearl into the thrusting channel, from bottom to top, then back down to the perineum. Repeat this pattern nine to eighteen times.
   Utilize your breath to enhance the effect of this meditation. When the pearl is in the perineum, inhale as you move it up the channel and exhale when moving down the channel. The breathing should be gentle and at normal pace.

Finish this section by moving the pearl into the cauldron, spiral and store it.

Part 4

The next channel is the Belt, Girdle or Dai channel, it wraps around the body like an energy belt and extends from below your feet to above your head, Figure 7b.

1. Move the pearl a few feet below your feet and spiral it clockwise nine times; finish this stage by drawing an energetic line from front to back and side to side of the circle (see below).

Front

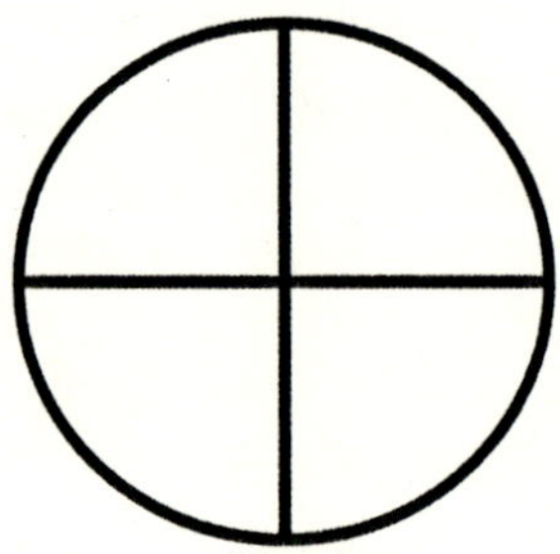

Back

2. Move the the pearl to the level of the feet and spiral it clockwise nine times; finish this stage by drawing an energetic line from front to back and side to side of the circle.
3. Move the pearl to the level of the knees and spiral it clockwise nine times; finish this stage by drawing an energetic line from front to back and side to side of the circle.
4. Move the pearl to the level of the perineum and spiral it in a clockwise flow nine times; finish this stage by drawing an energetic line from front to back and side to side of the circle.
5. Move the pearl to the level of the navel and circulate it around the waist in a clockwise flow. Circulate the pearl nine times at waist level, finish this stage by drawing an energetic line from front to back and side to side of the circle.

6. Move the pearl up to the solar plexus and circulate it nine times at this level in a clockwise flow; finish this stage by drawing an energetic line from front to back and side to side of the circle.
7. Move the pearl to the level of the Heart center and circulate it nine times in a clockwise flow, finish this stage by drawing an energetic line from front to back and side to side of the circle.
8. Move the pearl to the throat and circulate it nine times in a clockwise flow, finish this stage by drawing an energetic line from front to back and side to side of the circle.
9. Move the pearl to the level of the third eye, the area between the eyebrows and circulate the pearl nine times; finish this stage by drawing an energetic line from front to back and side to side of the circle.
10. Move the pearl to the level of the crown and spiral the pearl nine times; finish this stage by drawing an energetic line from front to back and side to side of the circle
11. Move the pearl a foot or more above the top of the head and spiral the pearl nine times in a clockwise flow; finish this stage by drawing an energetic line from front to back and side to side of the circle.
12. The next stage is moving the pearl down the body, when the pearl flows down it is circulated counter-clockwise.
13. Move the pearl to the levels of the crown, third eye, throat, Heart center, solar plexuses and navel, perineum, knees, feet and below the feet; at each stage spiral the pearl nine times stage spiral the pearl nine times in a counter-clockwise flow. Move in long, quick spirals down the body.
14. Spiral the pearl in a clockwise flow upward from below the feet to above the top of the head, then downward in a counter-clockwise flow from above the head to below the feet, each movement up and down represents one cycle. Perform this process nine or more times. Figure 7b.
15. End this stage by bringing the pearl inside the cauldron, spiral and store it.

Figure 7b

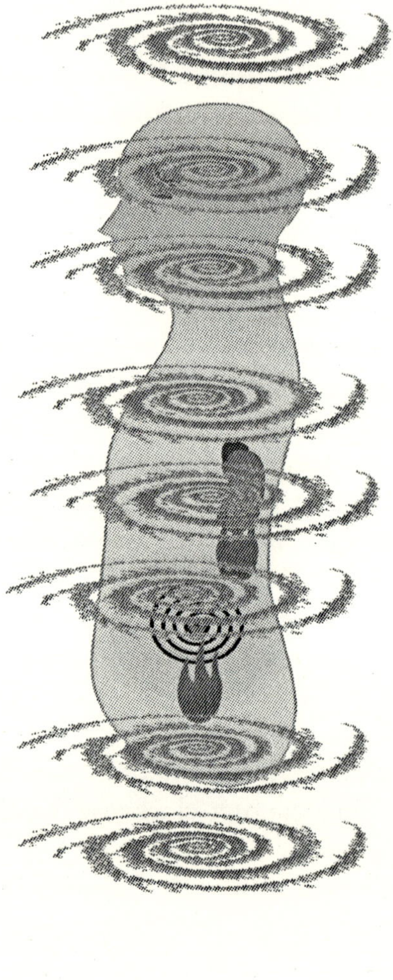

Part 5

1. This section includes the Yin and Yang aspects of the arms and legs, both inside and outside of the limbs; these are the Yin and Yang Wei and Yin and Yang Qiao channels.
2. Exhale while moving the pearl from the cauldron down to the perineum, split the pearl into two parts and move it down the inside the legs to the bottom of the feet.
3. Inhale while you move the pearl around the toes, up the sides of the legs to the waist, then to cervical vertebrae seven, the big bone between the shoulders, which is acupuncture point Du 14. This completes the inhale.
4. Exhale from Du 14 down the back of the arms to the fingers. This completes the exhale.
5. Inhale the pearl into the palm of the hands, up the inside of the arms to Du 14, up the neck to the top of the head. This completes the inhale.
6. Exhale the pearl down the front of the body, follow the nipple line to the perineum.
7. This represents one cycle, do this cycle nine times.
8. Finish this meditation by moving your attention and Qi into the cauldron, spiral and form the pearl.

This completes the Eight Treasures Qi Gong, it is a very profound meditation that clears these constitutional channels and refines one's energy and essence. These special energy channels comprise the "spiritual womb"; this cultivation prepares the womb for the immortal body formation and development. When practicing it is normal to feel very light and subtle, and a powerful connection to the Universe. This refinement process transcends the physical and emotional body; it is the entry to an expanded awareness of the spiritual body.

Chapter 8

Shen-Spirit Realization

Kan and Li Enlightenment

Turning inward reveals the essence and origin of the Universe.
The three treasures are the ingredients for transformation,
essence is the foundation,
energy generates vitality,
spirit is the offspring of the subtle realm.
Blend and refine the three treasures and the immortal spirit appears.

Look to Man and Woman, how do they create a new life?
by coupling their essences new life is created.
Can you couple Sun & Moon, Heaven & Earth, Water & Fire to create the immortal body.
This is the ancient secret revealed in Kan and Li!

Kan means Water, Li is Fire. Kan and Li Qi Gong cultivation is one of the ancient, esoteric, secret alchemy practices in the tradition of Tao. This process unifies Water-Fire, Yin-Yang, Moon-Sun, Female-Male, and Physical-Spiritual aspects of each person; it also reflects the integration of nature, a process creating life. Kan and Li culminate in an awareness and experience of eternal life; it is a formula for realizing one's true spiritual nature.

Kan and Li expands upon the eight extraordinary channel meditations; the process begins by expanding awareness of our integrated relationship with nature, particularly the Sun, Moon, Earth, Jupiter, Mars, Saturn, Venus and Mercury. In this cultivation we expand the usage of the cauldron, Figure 8a. The cauldron is an energetic transformer, it is in this location alchemy occurs that affects the body-mind-spirit or Jing-Qi-Shen. The goals of Kan and Li include:

- The Navel Center cultivation focuses on transforming Essence into Qi or vitality, expanding human consciousness into higher spiritual awareness, leading to transcending karmic conditioning from society, family and education. Essentially changing the karmic blueprint and releasing the natural, innate spiritual blueprint of life. Kan and Li cultivation of the Navel Center transcends the personal ego and reveals direct experience of the energy body. These practices initiate the process of overcoming the cycle of birth and death.
- The Solar Plexus Center cultivation focuses on integrating Universal Five Element correspondences and refining the pearl (the collective consciousness and essence of physical-emotional-spiritual life). This process expands awareness of the immortal spiritual body and unites personal consciousness and universal life.
- The Heart Center cultivation refines the pearl and awareness of the spiritual body. The spirit body transcends the dimensions of time and physical space and subtle Universal energies impregnate the spirit body; this is the spirit body receiving the "Immortal Pill or Elixir", unifying human consciousness and spiritual reality. Personal and subtle life are united and directly experienced.
- The Crystal Palace – Third Eye cultivation crystallizes the Five Shen and their related senses in the cauldron located in the primary spiritual center in the head. This process attracts very subtle Universal energies that grow the immortal spiritual body, leading to conscious unity with the subtle realm, Tao or God. This advanced cultivation harmonizes all centers or physical-mental-spiritual aspects of human life. The refined body is now able to absorb and assimilate these subtle energies, deepening the experience of one's true nature. Mastering this level leads to spiritual freedom.

The essence of this cultivation consists of two simultaneous phenomenon. The first consists of refining and increasing vitality or energy and the second is the transformation of consciousness. As one's energy is refined, their consciousness is refined; this refined consciousness is the immortal spirit or body. The eternal nature of human spirit always exists; our conscious awareness of it is developed, enhanced and retained when practicing Spiritual Qi Gong.

Spend one month to a year or more at each stage until you fully experience each process.

Figure 8a

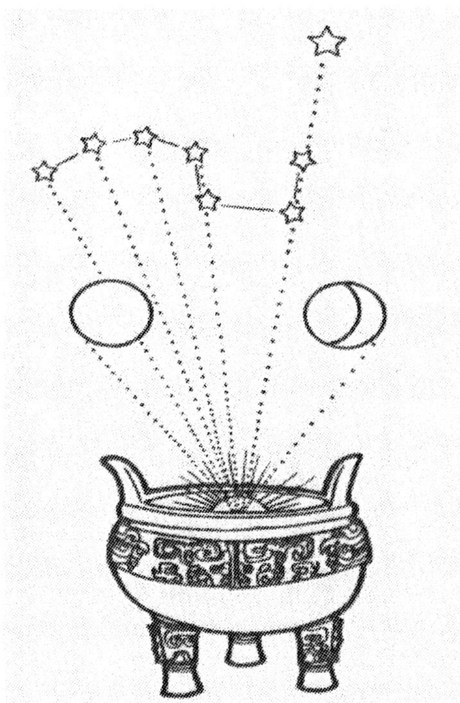

Shen-Spirit Realization
Navel Tan Tien Center

Shen Realization or Kan and Li cultivation begins by creating the cauldron in the lower Tan Tien (behind the navel). In this cauldron Essence or Jing is steamed creating Qi. This steaming releases enormous amounts of energy and vitalizes the body, particularly glands, organs, the brain and the nervous system. It also begins the process of transcending the physical body and resolving karmic conditions. The following is the process:

Part 1

1. Be aware of the cauldron behind the navel in the lower Tan Tien.
2. Focus your attention in the Kidneys, they are directly connected to the planet mercury, North direction, Water element and the Moon; be aware of these connections. Place your attention in the Moon above, gather this Yin essence from the Moon and place it into the Kidneys. Feel the cold-essence of the Kidneys; spend as much time as necessary to feel it. When there is a strong feeling move the essence and cold into the cauldron, spiral, collect and form the pearl.
3. Focus your attention in the adrenals and feel its Heat-Yang; the adrenals are located above the Kidneys. Place your attention in the Sun above, move the Yang essence of the Sun into the adrenals, when there is a strong Yang feeling move the Yang-heat underneath the cauldron, see and feel the Fire underneath the cauldron.
4. Feel the Yang-Fire heat up the cauldron and cook the Water-Yin-Cold-Essence. As the Yin-Essence heats up it begins to steam, this is the first goal, steaming the Essence. The fire must be strong enough to cook and steam the Yin-essence. This steaming process is a refinement of one's energy; it is transforming Essence-Jing into Qi-Vitality.

5. When steam appears guide it into the Kidneys, Liver, Pancreas, Spleen, Lungs, Heart, Thymus, Thyroid, Parathyroid, Pituitary and Pineal Glands, then the whole Brain. Follow the exact sequence for the steaming process. Spiral the steam in each area for 30 seconds to one minute.
6. Finish this stage by gathering the steam and guide it into the cauldron, spiral and collect it in the center of the cauldron and form it into the pearl. Spend as much time as necessary at each stage until you feel and experience each step.

Part 2

1. Continue from stage 1, guide the steam into the Orbit and circulate it 18-36 times; continue by guiding it through the Thrusting, Belt, Arm and Leg channels, 18-36 times.
2. Guide the steam through the 12 major internal organ channels. Please review any standard acupuncture book containing the basic channels for their pathways.
3. Focus your attention in the cauldron, feel the Yin-Essence inside and the Yang-Fire underneath, move the cauldron underneath the spine and feel the Yang-Fire cook the Yin-Essence, feel the essence cook and become steam, guide the steam into the spine and up into the brain; feel the steam move up and down the spine. Totally steaming the spine.
4. Guide the steam into the spine and spinal nerves. Spinal nerves connect to the whole body; feel steam spread through all nerves, organs, glands, skeletal, musculature and vascular systems.
5. Guide steam into the center of the cauldron, spiral and collect the steam-energy into the pearl.

Shen Realization
Solar Plexus Tan Tien Center

The goal of this cultivation is unification of the Five Shen, expanding the types of Universal energies gathered, absorbed and transformed, including Earth, Sun and Moon, and most importantly, conscious awareness and formation of the immortal spirit body.

Process

1. Be aware of the cauldron in the lower Tan Tien, move this cauldron to the level of the solar plexus. Spiral your attention in the cauldron and feel the pearl.
2. Be aware of the Kidneys, they are blue and reflect North, Water and the Will-Power/Zhi aspect of Shen-Spirit.
3. Be aware of the Heart, it is red and reflects South, Fire and Shen-Spirit.
4. Be aware of the Liver, it is green and reflects East, Wood and the ethereal, subtle aspect of our Spirit/Hun.
5. Be aware of the Lungs, they are white and reflect West, Metal and the corporeal aspect of our Spirit/Po.
6. Be aware of the Spleen, it is yellow and reflects the center, Earth, focus or concentration aspect of our Spirit/Yi.
7. Be aware of all these organs, their colors, directions and Spirit energy, guide their energy into the center of the cauldron, mixing, blending and integrating them to become a unified energy. This energy is the pearl; it is also the basis of the collective consciousness and essence or our body-mind-spirit.
8. When the pearl feels strong and vibrant, guide it into the Earth, deep into the center of the Earth. Feel mother Earth, the great healer and transformer, energize, transform and heal your pearl. Remember the pearl is the essence of your being, as the pearl

changes, you change. Stay in the Earth for five minutes or more. Ask the Earth to heal any aspects of your life that needs healing; ask the Earth to guide you in your life path. It will provide support to you.

9. Guide the pearl into the Orbit, then the Kidneys, Liver, Heart, Spleen, Lungs, Kidneys and back to the cauldron.
10. Be aware of the Sun and Moon above, move them side-by-side, then bring them down to the top of the head, guide them into the thrusting channel and to the top of the cauldron. Be aware of the pearl inside the cauldron, guide the Sun and Moon into the center of the cauldron and couple or blend their energies with the pearl. Spiral and blend all energies into one pearl. This coupled energy of the Sun-Yang-male and Moon-Yin-female energize and nourish the pearl and one's consciousness.
11. Feel the pearl nourished by the five organs, five shen, five directions, planet Earth and solar system.
12. Be aware of all forces, inside and out, energizing and nourishing the pearl. See the pearl take the form of an energy baby, a fully developed baby. Feel the energy baby nourished by the energy of the organs, Earth, Sun, Moon and solar system. Feel the energy baby grow stronger as nature and all Universal forces nourish it, Figurc 8b.
13. Consistent practice refines this pearl energy; this refined energy is a magnet attracting subtle energies from the Universe, this is called receiving the "Small Pill", the initial conscious experience of one's true immortal spiritual nature.

    End these meditations by focusing in the center, relax, breath naturally, smile and enjoy this experience.
14. The levels of experiencing this practice are vast, the more you refine your life, increased awareness and depth occur. Practice diligently until you feel the pearl radiant and the spiritual baby-body develop; with time and practice the subtle realm and its branches

will send the breath of immortal life and you will be prepared to receive and experience the Immortal Pill and your true nature.

15. As you master this level expand the practice by expanding the energy body to be the exact size as your physical body, feel the energy body radiant and experience the separation of the physical and energy body, actually it is experiencing transcending time and physical space. This energy body is your eternal life force; consciously experiencing this energy body is Shen Realization.

Figure 8b

Shen Realization
Heart Tan Tien Center

This practice includes expanding conscious awareness of the unification of the Five Shen and enhancing connections to the Sun, Moon and Five Planets. Universal vortexes: North Star and Big Dipper are absorbed and energize the immortal body; the immortal body-consciousness transcends the physical boundaries of time and space, achieving spiritual independence.

Move the cauldron into the Heart center. Be aware of the five organs, their colors, directions, energies and qualities; guide their energy into the center of the cauldron. Be aware of the Earth, Sun, Moon and entire solar system, guide their energy into the cauldron, feel the pearl nourished by all these Universal forces.

Be aware of the Sun above, focus your mind's attention (Yi) in the Sun, while inhaling guide the energy of the Sun into the Pineal Gland, when exhaling guide it back into the sky. Do this process 9 times or until you feel energy in the pineal gland.

Be aware of the Moon above; draw the Moon into the Pituitary Gland and to the location of the third eye, repeat the procedure used in step 2 with the Sun.

Feel the Sun and Moon above, move them side-by-side and guide them into the cauldron. Couple them in the cauldron with the pearl.

Feel the pearl in the cauldron and see it take the form of an energy body (figure 8b), feel all Universal energies nourish it. Feel the connection with Starry Beings: planets, stars and directional forces, merge with them. Spend as much time as necessary to feel this.

During this stage you may feel or see a light energize the energy-spirit body, this process is called receiving the " Immortal Elixir", " Divine Child" or " Big Pill", it is the subtle realm's immortal life force entering the immortal body, creating an awareness that you are both a dependent and independent immortal child. It is referred to as the "Red Baby" in ancient texts. It is the simultaneous conscious awareness and experience of your divine nature.

Focus on this energy body and expand it to reach your physical size, once you feel this move the energy body outside of your physical body, above your head, it is an exact replica of your physical body, now positioned above your head.

When you feel this energy body radiant and strong, move it into the solar system and merge with the Big Dipper, North Star and Starry Beings. Spend as much time at this stage or any stage until you feel the qualities discussed. Many of these meditations take time and practice, if you do not feel energy or the described qualities, finish the mediation and practice later or the next day, this is the cultivation process. Cultivation takes time and practice; it is an ongoing process that requires patience, dedication and gentleness.

When you are ready guide the energy body to the top of the head, into the physical body and then contract it into the pearl. Circulate the pearl though the Orbit nine times and then into the Kidneys, Liver, Heart, Spleen and Lungs nine times. End the meditation by bringing the pearl into the cauldron, spiral and collect it in the center of the cauldron.

Shen Realization
Third Eye Tan Tien Center

The subtle realm nurtures its offspring.
The Sun, Moon, North Star and Big Dipper,
mothers of human life nourish the spiritual baby.
Look to the East, South, North, West and Center.
fathers of the five shen nourish the spiritual baby.
Close the portals and unite Mother and Father,
individual spirit unites with the subtle realm creating Heaven in Earth.

The Third Eye Center or Crystal Palace is an area in the head that is behind the third eye, at the level of the apex of the ears, this area includes the pituitary and pineal glands. This location is referred to as the upper Tan Tien and is a high spiritual location in the human body. A high level of refinement is necessary to cultivate in this area, a person's awareness and energy must be refined to be able to absorb and digest Universal energies. In Alchemy, the head includes portals for all aspects of the spirit, Table 9a summarizes portals and their relationships.

This Qi Gong cultivation crystallizes the Five Shen and their sensory portals in the Crystal Palace, the residence of the pituitary and pineal glands; they are spiritual compasses and potent transmitters of spiritual energy. This cultivation unifies all centers and expands conscious awareness of the spiritual immortal body and its undivided relationships with the source of life. Living in the Tao or God consciousness becomes a daily reality in this practice.

Table 9a

Portal	Aspect of Spirit	Organ
Right Eye	Moon, Ethereal, Hun Spirit	Liver
Left Eye	Sun, Hun, Ethereal Spirit	Liver
Nose	Po, Corporeal Spirit	Lungs
Ears	Zhi, Will Power	Kidneys
Mouth	I, Focus	Spleen
Tongue	Shen, Spirit	Heart

The process

1. Be aware of the cauldron in the lower Tan Tien, behind the navel, feel all the organ's energies and the five shen beam into the center of the cauldron; feel the Earth, Sun, Moon and the entire solar system beam their energy into the cauldron, nourishing the pearl.
2. Repeat this process for the cauldron and the pearl at the level of the solar plexuses and Heart center.
3. Move the cauldron to the crystal palace and be aware of the pearl in the cauldron. See the Moon in the right eye and the Sun in the left eye, draw their energy into the cauldron.
4. Be aware of the mouth, connect the I-Spleen to the mouth and draw its energy into the cauldron.
5. Be aware of the ears, connect the Zhi-Kidneys to the ears and draw its energy into the cauldron.
6. Be aware of the tongue, connect the Shen-Heart to the tongue and draw its energy into the cauldron.
7. Be aware of the nose, connect the Po-Lungs to the nose and draw its energy into the cauldron.
8. Be aware of the eyes, connect the Hun-Liver to the eyes and draw the energy into the cauldron.

9. Be aware of the eyes, ears, nose, tongue and mouth and their respective organs and energies and draw their energy into the cauldron, nourishing the pearl.
10. Be aware of the North Star and Big Dipper, draw energy from the Big Dipper and North Star into the cauldron nourishing the pearl.
11. Be aware of the four cauldrons: navel, solar plexus, Heart and crystal palace centers, feel them radiate.
12. Move all your focus into the cauldron at the level of the solar plexus, transform the pearl into the energy body, draw energies from the solar system, Sun, Moon, Earth and the five organs into the cauldron, nourishing the energy body. Expand the energy body to become the same size as your physical body. Relax in this conscious state of bliss and joy, this is experiencing one's true spiritual nature, it is the fruit of Spiritual Qi Gong and Kan and Li cultivation. Consistent practice leads to deeper levels of awareness of this unity, creating a new dimension for experiencing daily life. The highest achievement is applying this experience into normal, regular daily life.

As your energy becomes refined you can absorb subtler energies from the Universe, you will feel your physical, energy and spirit bodies become lighter and lighter and transcend the dimensions of time and physical space. This transformation reveals your true nature, an immortal spirit that is inseparable from the source of life. This unification allows you to consciously realize your eternal union with the source of life, creator, Tao or God.

Conclusion

Spiritual Qi Gong is an ancient Taoist path to realizing one's true nature. People of all religions and philosophical traditions can practice Qi Gong; it embraces all people who pursue health, as well as the quest of knowing their true spiritual nature. These are gentle meditations that transform human consciousness, with consistent practice you will taste the fruit experienced by men and women for thousands of years. Please enjoy these ancient Qi Gong practices for Health, Longevity and Self-Realization.

Best Wishes,

David Twicken, Ph.D., L.Ac.

Zen Mountain Center
Mountain Center, California
January 1, 2001
Year of the Golden Dragon

Appendix

Introduction to the Chinese Calendar

The Chinese Calendar Made Easy © contains the information to find the five element energies for an hour, day, month and year. The following example illustrates how to calculate these energies. Use the information below or refer to 1999 in the Appendix.

A Male born January 28, 1999 at 5:30 am.

1999

Find your Day Here	Month Stem	Month Branch	Year Stem	Year Branch	Day	Day	Time
January 6 – February 4	Yin Wood	Ox	Yang Earth	Tiger	Jan	49	3: 00
February 4— March 6	Yang Fire	Tiger	Yin Earth	Rabbit	Feb	20	14: 42
March 6 —April 5	Yin Fire	Rabbit	Yin Earth	Rabbit	March	48	8: 52
April 5— May 6	Yang Earth	Dragon	Yin Earth	Rabbit	April	19	13: 55
May 6 – June 6	Yin Earth	Snake	Yin Earth	Rabbit	May	49	7: 29
June 6— July 7	Yang Metal	Horse	Yin Earth	Rabbit	June	20	11: 51
July 7— August 8	Yin Metal	Sheep	Yin Earth	Rabbit	July	50	22: 14
August 8— September 8	Yang Water	Monkey	Yin Earth	Rabbit	Aug	21	7: 57
September 8 – October 9	Yin Water	Cock	Yin Earth	Rabbit	Sept	52	10: 41
October 9— November 7	Yang Wood	Dog	Yin Earth	Rabbit	Oct	22	2: 05
November 7— December 7	Yin Wood	Pig	Yin Earth	Rabbit	Nov	53	5: 01
December 7 – January 6	Yang Fire	Rat	Yin Earth	Rabbit	Dec	23	21: 14

1. Locate the solar day in column 1.
   Move directly to the right and take note of the Month Stem and Branch, in this example Column 2 or Yin Wood, Ox. Place this Binomial in the Four Pillar Chart below.

	Hour	Day	Month	Year
Stem			**Yin Wood**	
Branch			**Ox**	

2. Move directly to the right and write down the Year Stem and Branch. Column 3. Yang Earth, Tiger. See Four Pillars below.

	Hour	Day	Month	Year
Stem			Yin Wood	Yang Earth
Branch			Ox	Tiger

3. Move to the right and locate the month in question, January (column 4) and continue to the right to the Day number, take note of the number in the Day Column, Column 5.

   Add the day of birth on any day to this number. 49 plus 28 (January 28) = 77. 77-60 = *17,* this is the Day Stem and Branch Binomial.

The number in this column assists in finding the Binomial for the Day of birth. There are 60 Binomials or combinations. If the total of the Birthday and the Column Day exceeds 60, subtract 60 from the total. In this example, the total is 77, subtract 60, resulting in Binomial 17.

In the Stem and Branch Cycle of 60 Chart below, find Binomial *17,* this is the Day Stem and Branch Binomial. It is Yang Metal, Dragon. Place this Binomial in the Four Pillars.

	Hour	Day	Month	Year
Stem		Yang Metal	Yin Wood	Yang Earth
Branch		Dragon	Ox	Tiger

Stem and Branch Cycle of 60 Hours, Days, Months and Years

Number Stem Branch	1 Yang Wood Rat	2 Yin Wood Ox	3 Yang Fire Tiger	4 Yin Fire Rabbit	5 Yang Earth Dragon	6 Yin Earth Snake
Number Stem Branch	7 Yang Metal Horse	8 Yin Metal Sheep	9 Yang Water Monkey	10 Yin Water Cock	11 Yang Wood Dog	12 Yin Wood Pig
Number Stem Branch	13 Yang Fire Rat	14 Yin Fire Ox	15 Yang Earth Tiger	16 Yin Earth Rabbit	17 Yang Metal Dragon	18 Yin Metal Snake
Number Stem Branch	19 Yang Water Horse	20 Yin Water Sheep	21 Yang Wood Monkey	22 Yin Wood Cock	23 Yang Fire Dog	24 Yin Fire Pig
Number Stem Branch	25 Yang Earth Rat	26 Yin Earth Ox	27 Yang Metal Tiger	28 Yin Metal Rabbit	29 Yang Water Dragon	30 Yin Water Snake
Number Stem Branch	31 Yang Wood Horse	32 Yin Wood Sheep	33 Yang Fire Monkey	34 Yin Fire Cock	35 Yang Earth Dog	36 Yin Earth Pig
Number Stem Branch	37 Yang Metal Rat	38 Yin Metal Ox	39 Yang Water Tiger	40 Yin Water Rabbit	41 Yang Wood Dragon	42 Yin Wood Snake
Number Stem Branch	43 Yang Fire Horse	44 Yin Fire Sheep	45 Yang Earth Monkey	46 Yin Earth Cock	47 Yang Metal Dog	48 Yin Metal Pig
Number Stem Branch	49 Yang Water Rat	50 Yin Water Ox	51 Yang Wood Tiger	52 Yin Wood Rabbit	53 Yang Fire Dragon	54 Yin Fire Snake
Number Stem Branch	55 Yang Earth Horse	56 Yin Earth Sheep	57 Yang Metal Monkey	58 Yin Metal Cock	59 Yang Water Dog	60 Yin Water Pig

Branch	Pig	Rat	Ox	Tiger	Rabbit	Dragon	Snake	Horse	Sheep	Monkey	Cock	Dog
Main Element	Yang Water	Yin Water	Yin Earth	Yang Wood	Yin Wood	Yang Earth	Yang Fire	Yin Fire	Yin Earth	Yang Metal	Yin Metal	Yang Earth

4. Refer to the Hour Stem and Branch Chart below; locate the *Day Stem* in the top row and look directly below it to the Stem and Branch that corresponds to the time of birth. The Day Stem is Yang Metal, move to 5:30 am which is Yin Earth, Rabbit. This is the Hour Stem and Branch. See below.

Hour Stem and Branch Chart

Day Stem →	Yang Wood Yin Earth	Yang Metal Yin Wood	Yang Fire Yin Metal	Yang Water Yin Fire	Yang Earth Yin Water
11 pm-1 am	Yang Wood Rat	Yang Fire Rat	Yang Earth Rat	Yang Metal Rat	Yang Water Rat
1 am-3 am	Yin Wood Ox	Yin Fire Ox	Yin Earth Ox	Yin Metal Ox	Yin Water Ox
3 am-5 am	Yang Fire Tiger	Yang Earth Tiger	Yang Metal Tiger	Yang Water Tiger	Yang Wood Tiger
5 am-7 am	Yin Fire Rabbit	Yin Earth Rabbit	Yin Metal Rabbit	Yin Water Rabbit	Yin Wood Rabbit
7 am-9 am	Yang Earth Dragon	Yang Metal Dragon	Yang Water Dragon	Yang Wood Dragon	Yang Fire Dragon
9 am-11 am	Yin Earth Snake	Yin Metal Snake	Yin Water Snake	Yin Wood Snake	Yin Fire Snake
11 am-1 pm	Yang Metal Horse	Yang Water Horse	Yang Wood Horse	Yang Fire Horse	Yang Earth Horse
1 pm-3 pm	Yin Metal Sheep	Yin Water Sheep	Yin Wood Sheep	Yin Fire Sheep	Yin Earth Sheep
3 pm-5 pm	Yang Water Monkey	Yang Wood Monkey	Yang Fire Monkey	Yang Earth Monkey	Yang Metal Monkey
5 pm-7 pm	Yin Water Cock	Yin Wood Cock	Yin Fire Cock	Yin Earth Cock	Yin Metal Cock
7 pm- 9 pm	Yang Wood Dog	Yang Fire Dog	Yang Earth Dog	Yang Metal Dog	Yang Water Dog
9 pm-11 pm	Yin Wood Pig	Yin Fire Pig	Yin Earth Pig	Yin Metal Pig	Yin Water Pig

	Hour	Day	Month	Year
Stem	Yin Earth	Yang Metal	Yin Wood	Yang Earth
Branch	Rabbit	Dragon	Ox	Tiger

Chinese Calendar

Made Easy ©

Years 1920-2010

by

David Twicken, Ph.D., L.Ac.

1921

Find your Day Here	Month Stem	Month Branch	Year Stem	Year Branch	Day	Day	Time
February 4 — March 6	Yang Metal	Tiger	Yin Metal	Cock	Feb	31	16:21
March 6 — April 5	Yin Metal	Rabbit	Yin Metal	Cock	Mar	59	10:36
April 5 — May 6	Yang Water	Dragon	Yin Metal	Cock	April	30	16:03
May 6 – June 6	Yin Water	Sna ke	Yin Metal	Cock	May	0	10:06
June 6 — July 8	Yang Wood	Horse	Yin Metal	Cock	June	31	14:51
July 8 — August 8	Yin Wood	Sheep	Yin Metal	Cock	July	1	1:24
August 8 — September 8	Yang Fire	Monkey	Yin Metal	Cock	Aug	32	11:17
September 8 – October 9	Yin Fire	Cock	Yin Metal	Cock	Sep	3	14:04
October 9 — November 8	Yang Earth	Dog	Yin Metal	Cock	Oct	33	5:22
November 8 — December 7	Yin Earth	Pig	Yin Metal	Cock	Nov	4	7:58
December 7 – January 6	Yang Metal	Rat	Yin Metal	Cock	Dec	34	0:07

Branch	Pig	Rat	Ox	Tiger	Rabbit	Dragon	Snake	Horse	Sheep	Monk ey	Cock	Dog
Main Element	Yang Water	Yin Water	Yin Earth	Yang Wood	Yin Wood	Yang Earth	Yang Fire	Yin Fire	Yin Earth	Yang Metal	Yin Metal	Yang Earth
Hidden Elements	Yang Wood		Yin Water Yin Metal	Yang Fire Yang Earth		Yin Wood Yin Water	Yang Earth Yang Metal	Yin Earth	Yin Fire Yin Wood	Yang Earth Yang Water		Yin Metal Yin Fire

1922

Find your Day Here	Month Stem	Month Branch	Year Stem	Year Branch	Day	Day	Time
January 6 – February 4	Yin Metal	Ox	Yin Metal	Cock	Jan	5	10:42
February 4— March 6	Yang Water	Tiger	Yang Water	Dog	Feb	36	22:09
March 6— April 5	Yin Water	Rabbit	Yang Water	Dog	Mar	4	16:25
April 5— May 6	Yang Wood	Dragon	Yang Water	Dog	April	35	21:52
May 6 – June 6	Yin Wood	Snake	Yang Water	Dog	May	5	15:55
June 6— July 8	Yang Fire	Horse	Yang Water	Dog	June	36	20:40
July 8- August 8	Yin Fire	Sheep	Yang Water	Dog	July	6	7:13
August 8— September 8	Yang Earth	Monkey	Yang Water	Dog	Aug	37	17:05
September 8 – October 9	Yin Earth	Cock	Yang Water	Dog	Sep	8	19:52
October 9— November 8	Yang Metal	Dog	Yang Water	Dog	Oct	38	11:11
November 8- December 8	Yin Metal	Pig	Yang Water	Dog	Nov	9	13:47
December 8 – January 6	Yang Water	Rat	Yang Water	Dog	Dec	39	5:57

1923

Find your Day Here	Month Stem	Month Branch	Year Stem	Year Branch	Day	Day	Time
January 6 – February 5	Yin Water	Ox	Yang Water	Dog	Jan	10	16:33
February 5— March 6	Yang Wood	Tiger	Yin Water	Pig	Feb	41	3:58
March 6— April 6	Yin Wood	Rabbit	Yin Water	Pig	Mar	9	22:25
April 6— May 6	Yang Fire	Dragon	Yin Water	Pig	April	40	21:41
May 6 – June 6	Yin Fire	Snake	Yin Water	Pig	May	10	21:28
June 7— July 8	Yang Earth	Horse	Yin Water	Pig	June	41	2:27
July 8— August 8	Yin Earth	Sh eep	Yin Water	Pig	July	11	13:01
August 8— September 9	Yang Metal	Monkey	Yin Water	Pig	Aug	42	22:53
September 9 – October 9	Yin Metal	Cock	Yin Water	Pig	Sep	13	1:41
October 9— November 8	Yang Water	Dog	Yin Water	Pig	Oct	43	17:00
November 8— December 8	Yin Water	Pig	Yin Water	Pig	Nov	14	19:30
December 8 – January 6	Yang Wood	Rat	Yin Water	Pig	Dec	44	11:47

Branch	Pig	Rat	Ox	Tiger	Rabbit	Dragon	Snake	Horse	Sheep	Monkey	Cock	Dog
Main Element	Yang Water	Yin Water	Yin Earth	Yang Wood	Yin Wood	Yang Earth	Yang Fire	Yin Fire	Yin Earth	Yang Metal	Yin Metal	Yang Earth
Hidden Elements	Yang Wood		Yin Water Yin Metal	Yang Fire Yang Earth		Yin Wood Yin Water	Yang Earth Yang Metal	Yin Earth	Yin Fire Yin Wood	Yang Earth Yang Water		Yin Metal Yin Fire

1924

Find your Day Here	Month Stem	Month Branch	Year Stem	Year Branch	Day	Day	Time
January 6 – February 5	Yin Wood	Ox	Yin Water	Pig	Jan	15	22:24
February 5-29— March 6	Yang Fire	Tiger	Yang Wood	Rat	Feb	46	9:49
March 6— April 5	Yin Fire	Rabbit	Yang Wood	Rat	Mar	15	4:13
April 5— May 6	Yang Earth	Dragon	Yang Wood	Rat	April	46	9:34
May 6 – June 6	Yin Earth	Snake	Yang Wood	Rat	May	16	3:26
June 6— July 7	Yang Metal	Horse	Yang Wood	Rat	June	47	8:02
July 7— August 8	Yin Metal	Sheep	Yang Wood	Rat	July	17	18:30
August 8— September 8	Yang Water	Monkey	Yang Wood	Rat	Aug	48	4:13
September 8 – October 8	Yin Water	Cock	Yang Wood	Rat	Sep	19	6:46
October 8— November 8	Yang Wood	Dog	Yang Wood	Rat	Oct	49	9:53
November 8— December 7	Yin Wood	Pig	Yang Wood	Rat	Nov	20	:30
December 7 – January 6	Yang Fire	Rat	Yang Wood	Rat	Dec	50	16:54

1925

Find your Day Here	Month Stem	Month Branch	Year Stem	Year Branch	Day	Day	Time
January 6 – February 4	Yin Fire	Ox	Yang Wood	Rat	Jan	21	3:54
February 4— March 6	Yang Earth	Tiger	Yin Wood	Ox	Feb	52	15:37
March 6— April 5	Yin Earth	Rabbit	Yin Wood	Ox	Mar	20	10:00
April 5— May 6	Yang Metal	Dragon	Yin Wood	Ox	April	51	15:23
May 6 – June 6	Yin Metal	Snake	Yin Wood	Ox	May	21	9:18
June 6— July 8	Yang Water	Horse	Yin Wood	Ox	June	52	13:5 7
July 8— August 8	Yin Water	Sheep	Yin Wood	Ox	July	22	0:25
August 8— September 7	Yang Wood	Monkey	Yin Wood	Ox	Aug	53	10:08
September 8 – October 9	Yin Wood	Cock	Yin Wood	Ox	Sep	24	12:40
October 9— November 8	Yang Fire	Dog	Yin Wood	Ox	Oct	54	3:48
November 8— December 7	Yin Fire	Pig	Yin Wood	Ox	Nov	25	6:27
December 7 – January 6	Yang Earth	Rat	Yin Wood	Ox	Dec	55	22:53

Branch	Pig	Rat	Ox	Tiger	Rabbit	Dragon	Snake	Horse	Sheep	Monkey	Cock	Dog
Main Element	Yang Water	Yin Water	Yin Earth	Yang Wood	Yin Wood	Yang Earth	Yang Fire	Yin Fire	Yin Earth	Yang Metal	Yin Metal	Yang Earth
Hidden Elements	Yang Wood		Yin Water Yin Metal	Yang Fire Yang Earth		Yin Wood Yin Water	Yang Earth Yang Metal	Yin Earth	Yin Fire Yin Wood	Yang Earth Yang Water		Yin Meta l Yin Fire

1926

Find your Day Here	Month		Year				
	Stem	Branch	Stem	Branch	Day	Day	Time
January 6 – February 4	Yin Earth	Ox	Yin Wood	Ox	Jan	26	9:55
February 4— March 6	Yang Metal	Tiger	Yang Fire	Tiger	Feb	57	21:39
March 6— April 5	Yin Metal	Rabbit	Yang Fire	Tiger	Mar	25	15:49
April 5— May 6	Yang Water	Dragon	Yang Fire	Tiger	April	56	21:19
May 6– June 6	Yin Water	Snake	Yang Fire	Tiger	May	26	15:09
June 6— July 8	Yang Wood	Horse	Yang Fire	Tiger	June	57	19:42
July 8— August 8	Yin Wood	Sheep	Yang Fire	Tiger	July	27	6:06
August 8— September 8	Yang Fire	Monkey	Yang Fire	Tiger	Aug	58	15:45
September 8 – October 9	Yin Fire	Cock	Yang Fire	Tiger	Sep	29	18:16
October 9— November 8	Yang Earth	Dog	Yang Fire	Tiger	Oct	59	9:25
November 8— December 8	Yin Earth	Pig	Yang Fire	Tiger	Nov	30	12:08
December 8 – January 6	Yang Metal	Rat	Yang Fire	Tiger	Dec	60	4:39

1927

Find your Day Here	Month		Year				
	Stem	Branch	Stem	Branch	Day	Day	Time
January 6 – February 5	Yin Metal	Ox	Yang Fire	Tiger	Jan	31	15:45
February 5— March 6	Yang Water	Tiger	Yin Fire	Rabbit	Feb	2	3:10
March 6— April 6	Yin Water	Rabbit	Yin Fire	Rabbit	Mar	30	21:51
April 6— May 6	Yang Wood	Dragon	Yin Fire	Rabbit	April	1	3:07
May 6 – June 7	Yin Wood	Snake	Yin Fire	Rabbit	May	31	20:54
June 7— July 8	Yang Fire	Horse	Yin Fire	Rabbit	June	2	1:25
July 8— August 8	Yin Fire	Sheep	Yin Fire	Rabbit	July	32	11:50
August 8— September 8	Yang Earth	Monkey	Yin Fire	Rabbit	Aug	3	21:32
September 8 – October 9	Yin Earth	Cock	Yin Fire	Rabbit	Sep	34	0:06
October 9— November 8	Yang Metal	Dog	Yin Fire	Rabbit	Oct	4	15:16
November 8— December 8	Yin Metal	Pig	Yin Fire	Rabbit	Nov	35	17:57
December 8 – January 6	Yang Water	Rat	Yin Fire	Rabbit	Dec	5	10:27

Branch	Pig	Rat	Ox	Tiger	Rabbit	Dragon	Snake	Horse	Sheep	Monkey	Cock	Dog
Main Element	Yang Water	Yin Water	Yin Earth	Yang Wood	Yin Wood	Yang Earth	Yang Fire	Yin Fire	Yin Earth	Yang Metal	Yin Metal	Yang Earth
Hidden Elements	Yang Wood		Yin Water Yin Metal	Yang Fire Yang Earth		Yin Wood Yin Water	Yang Earth Yang Metal	Yin Earth	Yin Fire Yin Wood	Yang Earth Yang Water		Yin Metal Yin Fire

1928

Find your Day Here	Month Stem	Month Branch	Year Stem	Year Branch	Day	Day	Time
January 6 – February 5	Yin Water	Ox	Yin Fire	Rabbit	Jan	36	21:32
February 5-29— March 6	Yang Wood	Tiger	Yang Earth	Dragon	Feb	7	9:17
March 6— April 5	Yin Wood	Rabbit	Yang Earth	Dragon	Mar	36	3:38
April 5— May 6	Yang Fire	Dragon	Yang Earth	Dragon	April	7	8:55
May 6 – June 6	Yin Fire	Snake	Yang Earth	Dragon	May	37	2:44
June 6— July 7	Yang Earth	Horse	Yang Earth	Dragon	June	8	7:18
July 7— August 8	Yin Earth	Sheep	Yang Earth	Drago n	July	38	17:45
August 8— September 8	Yang Metal	Monkey	Yang Earth	Dragon	Aug	9	3:28
September 8 – October 8	Yin Metal	Cock	Yang Earth	Dragon	Sep	40	6:02
October 8— November 7	Yang Water	Dog	Yang Earth	Dragon	Oct	10	21:11
November 7— December 7	Yin Water	Pig	Yang Earth	Dragon	Nov	41	23:50
December 7 – January 6	Yang Wood	Rat	Yang Earth	Dragon	Dec	11	16:18

1929

Find your Day Here	Month Stem	Month Branch	Year Stem	Year Branch	Day	Day	Time
January 6 – February 4	Yin Wood	Ox	Yang Earth	Dragon	Jan	42	3:23
February 4— March 6	Yang Fire	Tiger	Yin Earth	Snake	Feb	13	15:09
March 6— April 5	Yin Fire	Rabbit	Yin Earth	Snake	Mar	41	9:32
April 5— May 6	Yang Earth	Dragon	Yin Earth	Snake	April	12	14:52
May 6 – June 6	Yin Earth	Snake	Yin Earth	Snake	May	42	8:41
June 6— July 7	Yang Metal	Horse	Yin Earth	Snake	June	13	13:11
July 7— August 8	Yin Metal	Sheep	Yin Earth	Snake	July	43	23:32
August 8— September 8	Yang Water	Monkey	Yin Earth	Snake	Aug	14	9:09
September 8 – October 9	Yin Water	Cock	Yin Earth	Snake	Sep	45	11:40
October 9— November 8	Yang Wood	Dog	Yin Earth	Snake	Oct	15	2:48
November 8— December 7	Yin Wood	Pig	Yin Earth	Snake	Nov	46	5:28
December 7 – January 6	Yang Fire	Rat	Yin Earth	Snake	Dec	16	21:57

Branch	Pig	Rat	Ox	Tiger	Rabbit	Dragon	Snake	Horse	Sheep	Monkey	Cock	Dog
Main Element	Yang Water	Yin Water	Yin Earth	Yang Wood	Yin Wood	Yang Earth	Yang Fire	Yin Fire	Yin Earth	Yang Metal	Yin Metal	Yang Earth
Hidden Elements	Yang Wood		Yin Water Yin Metal	Yang Fire Yang Earth		Yin Wood Yin Water	Yang Earth Yang Metal	Yin Earth	Yin Fire Yin Wood	Yang Earth Yang Water		Yin Metal Yin Fire

1930

Find Your Day Here	Month Stem	Month Branch	Year Stem	Year Branch	Day	Day	Time
January 6 – February 4	Yin Fire	Ox	Yin Earth	Snake	Jan	47	9: 03
February 4— March 6	Yang Earth	Tiger	Yang Metal	Horse	Feb	18	20: 52
March 6— April 5	Yin Earth	Rabbit	Yang Metal	Horse	Mar	46	15: 17
April 5— May 6	Yang Metal	Dragon	Yang Metal	Horse	April	17	20: 38
May 6– June 6	Yin Metal	Snake	Yang Metal	Horse	May	47	14: 28
June 6— July 8	Yang Water	Horse	Yang Metal	Horse	June	18	18: 58
July 8— August 8	Yin Water	Sheep	Yang Metal	Horse	July	48	5: 20
August 8— September 8	Yang Wood	Monkey	Yang Metal	Horse	Aug	19	14: 58
September 8 – October 9	Yin Wood	Cock	Yang Metal	Horse	Sep	50	17:29
October 9— November 8	Yang Fire	Dog	Yang Metal	Hors e	Oct	20	8:38
November 8— December 8	Yin Fire	Pig	Yang Metal	Horse	Nov	51	11: 21
December 8 – January 6	Yang Earth	Rat	Yang Metal	Horse	Dec	21	3:51

1931

Find Your Day Here	Month Stem	Month Branch	Year Stem	Year Branch	Day	Day	Time
January 6 – February 5	Yin Earth	Ox	Yang Metal	Horse	Jan	52	14:56
February 5— March 6	Yang Metal	Tiger	Yin Metal	Sheep	Feb	23	2: 41
March 6— April 6	Yin Metal	Rabbit	Yin Metal	Sheep	Mar	51	21: 03
April 6— May 6	Yang Water	Dragon	Yin Metal	Sheep	April	22	2: 21
May 6 – June 7	Yin Water	Snake	Yin Metal	Sheep	May	52	20: 10
June 7— July 8	Yang Wood	Horse	Yin Metal	Sheep	June	23	: 42
July 8— August 8	Yin Wood	Sheep	Yin Metal	Sheep	July	53	11: 06
August 8— September 8	Yang Fire	Monkey	Yin Metal	Sheep	Aug	24	20: 45
September 8 – October 9	Yin Fire	Cock	Yin Metal	Sheep	Sep	55	23:18
October 9— November 8	Yang Earth	Dog	Yin Metal	Sheep	Oct	25	14:27
November 8— December 8	Yin Earth	Pig	Yin Metal	Sheep	Nov	56	17: 10
December 8 – January 6	Yang Metal	Rat	Yin Metal	Sheep	Dec	26	9: 41

Branch	Pig	Rat	Ox	Tiger	Rabbit	Dragon	Snake	Horse	Sheep	Monkey	Cock	Dog
Main Element	Yang Water	Yin Water	Yin Earth	Yang Wood	Yin Wood	Yang Earth	Yang Fire	Yin Fire	Yin Earth	Yang Metal	Yin Metal	Yang Earth
Hidden Elements	Yang Wood		Yin Water Yin Metal	Yang Fire Yang Earth		Yin Wood Yin Water	Yang Earth Yang Metal	Yin Earth	Yin Fire Yin Wood	Yang Earth Yang Water		Yin Metal Yin Fire

1932

Find Your Day Here	Month Stem	Month Branch	Year Stem	Year Branch	Day	Day	Time
January 6– February 5	Yin Metal	Ox	Yin Metal	Sheep	Jan	57	20:46
February 5-29, — March 6	Yang Water	Tiger	Yang Water	Monkey	Feb	28	8:30
March 6— April 5	Yin Water	Rabbit	Yang Water	Monkey	Mar	57	2:50
April 5— May 6	Yang Wood	Dragon	Yang Water	Monkey	April	28	8:07
May 6 – June 6	Yin Wood	Snake	Yang Water	Monkey	May	58	1:55
June 6— July 7	Yang Fire	Horse	Yang Water	Monkey	June	29	6:28
July 7— August 8	Yin Fire	Sheep	Yang Water	Monkey	July	59	16:53
August 8— September 8	Yang Earth	Monkey	Yang Water	Monkey	Aug	30	2:32
September 8 – October 8	Yin Earth	Cock	Yang Water	Monkey	Sep	1	5:03
October 8— November 7	Yang Meta	Dog	Yang Water	Monkey	Oct	31	20:10
November 7— December 7	Yin Metal	Pig	Yang Water	Monkey	Nov	2	22:50
December 7 – January 6	Yang Wate	Rat	Yang Water	Monkey	Dec	32	15:19

1933

Find Your Day Here	Month Stem	Month Branch	Year Stem	Year Branch	Day	Day	Time
January 6 – February 4	Yin Water	Ox	Yang Water	Monkey	Jan	57	2: 24
February 4 —March 6	Yang Wood	Tiger	Yin Water	Cock	Feb	28	14: 10
March 6 – April 5	Yin Wood	Rabbit	Yin Water	Cock	Mar	57	8: 32
April 5 – May 6	Yang Fire	Dragon	Yin Water	Cock	April	28	13: 51
May 6 – June 6	Yin Fire	Snake	Yin Water	Cock	May	58	7: 42
June 6 – July 7	Yang Earth	Horse	Yin Water	Cock	June	29	12: 18
July 7 – August 8	Yin Earth	Sheep	Yin Water	Cock	July	59	22: 45
August 8– September 8	Yang Metal	Monkey	Yin Water	Cock	Aug	30	8:26
September 8 – October 9	Yin Metal	Cock	Yin Water	Cock	Sep	1	10:58
October 9 – November 8	Yang Water	D og	Yin Water	Cock	Oct	31	2:08
November 8 – December 7	Yin Water	Pig	Yin Water	Cock	Nov	2	4:44
December 7 – January 6	Yang Wood	Rat	Yin Water	Cock	Dec	32	21:12

Branch	Pig	Rat	Ox	Tiger	Rabbit	Dragon	Snake	Horse	Sheep	Monkey	Cock	Dog
Main Element	Yang Water	Yin Water	Yin Earth	Yang Wood	Yin Wood	Yang Earth	Yang Fire	Yin Fire	Yin Earth	Yang Metal	Yin Metal	Yang Earth
Hidden Elements	Yang Wood		Yin Water Yin Metal	Yang Fire Yang Earth		Yin Wood Yin Water	Yang Earth Yang Metal	Yin Earth	Yin Fire Yin Wood	Yang Earth Yang Water		Yin Metal Yin Fire

1934

Find Your Day Here	Month Stem	Month Branch	Year Stem	Year Branch	Day	Day	Time
January 6– February 4	Yin Wood	Ox	Yin Water	Cock	Jan	8	8: 17
February 4— March 6	Yang Fire	Tiger	Yang Wood	Dog	Feb	39	20: 04
March 6— April 5	Yin Fire	Rabbit	Yang Wood	Dog	Mar	7	14: 27
April 5— May 6	Yang Earth	Dragon	Yang Wood	Dog	April	38	19: 44
May 6 – June 6	Yin Earth	Snake	Yang Wood	Dog	May	8	13: 31
June 6— July 8	Yang Metal	Horse	Yang Wood	Dog	June	39	18: 02
July 8— August 8	Yin Metal	Sheep	Yang Wood	Dog	July	9	4: 25
August 8— September 8	Yang Water	Monkey	Yang Wood	Dog	Aug	40	14:04
September 8 – October 9	Yin Water	Cock	Yang Wood	Dog	Sep	11	16: 37
October 9— November 8	Yang Wood	Dog	Yang Wood	Dog	Oct	41	7: 45
November 8— December 8	Yin Wood	Pig	Yang Wood	Dog	Nov	12	10: 27
December 8 – January 6	Yang Fire	Rat	Yang Wood	Dog	Dec	42	2:57

1935

Find your Day Here	Month Stem	Month Branch	Year Stem	Year Branch	Day	Day	Time
January 6– February 5	Yin Fire	Ox	Yang Wood	Dog	Jan	13	14: 03
February 5— March 6	Yang Earth	Tiger	Yin Wood	Pig	Feb	44	1: 49
March 6— April 6	Yin Earth	Rabbit	Yin Wood	Pig	Mar	12	20: 11
April 6— May 6	Yang Metal	Dragon	Yin Wood	Pig	April	43	1: 27
May 6– June 6	Yin Metal	Snake	Yin Wood	Pig	May	13	19:12
June 6— July 8	Yang Water	Horse	Yin Wood	Pig	June	44	23:42
July 8— August 8	Yin Water	Sheep	Yin Wood	Pig	July	14	10: 06
August 8— September 8	Yang Wood	Monkey	Yin Wood	Pig	Aug	45	19: 48
September 8 – October 9	Yin Wood	Cock	Yin Wood	Pig	Sep	16	22: 25
October 9— November 8	Yang Fire	Dog	Yin Wood	Pig	Oct	46	13: 36
November 8— December 8	Yin Fire	Pig	Yin Wood	Pig	Nov	17	16: 18
December 8 – January 6	Yang Earth	Rat	Yin Wood	Pig	Dec	47	8: 45

Branch	Pig	Rat	Ox	Tiger	Rabbit	Dragon	Snake	Horse	Sheep	Monkey	Cock	Dog
Main Element	Yang Water	Yin Water	Yin Earth	Yang Wood	Yin Wood	Yang Earth	Yang Fire	Yin Fire	Yin Earth	Yang Metal	Yin Metal	Yang Earth
Hidden Elements	Yang Wood		Yin Water Yin Metal	Yang Fire Yang Earth		Yin Wood Yin Water	Yang Earth Yang Metal	Yin Earth	Yin Fire Yin Wood	Yang Earth Yang Water		Yin Metal Yin Fire

1936

Find your Day Here	Month Stem	Month Branch	Year Stem	Year Branch	Day	Day	Time
January 6 – February 5	Yin Earth	Ox	Yin Wood	Pig	Jan	18	19: 47
February 5 – 29,— March 6	Yang Metal	Tiger	Yang Fire	Rat	Feb	49	7: 29
March 6— April 5	Yin Metal	Rabbit	Yang Fire	Rat	Mar	18	1: 50
April 5— May 6	Yang Water	Dragon	Yang Fire	Rat	April	49	7: 07
May 6 – June 6	Yin Water	Snake	Yang Fire	Rat	May	19	: 57
June 6— July 7	Yang Wood	Horse	Yang Fire	Rat	June	50	5: 31
July 7— August 8	Yin Wood	Sheep	Yang Fire	Rat	July	20	15: 59
August 8— September 8	Yang Fire	Monkey	Yang Fire	Rat	Aug	51	1: 43
September 8 – October 8	Yin Fire	Cock	Yang Fire	Rat	Sep	22	4:21
October 8— November 7	Yang Earth	Dog	Yang Fire	Rat	Oct	52	19: 33
November 7— December 7	Yin Earth	Pig	Yang Fire	Rat	Nov	23	22:15
December 7 – January 6	Yang Metal	Rat	Yang Fire	Rat	Dec	53	14:43

1937

Find your Day Here	Month Stem	Month Branch	Year Stem	Year Branch	Day	Day	Time
January 6— February 4	Yin Metal	Ox	Yang Fire	Rat	Jan	24	1: 44
February 4 —March 6	Yang Water	Tiger	Yin Fire	Ox	Feb	55	13: 26
March 6 – April 5	Yin Water	Rabbit	Yin Fire	Ox	Mar	23	7: 45
April 5 – May 6	Yang Wood	Dragon	Yin Fire	Ox	April	54	13: 02
May 6 – June 6	Yin Wood	Snake	Yin Fire	Ox	May	24	6: 51
June 6 – July 7	Yang Fire	Horse	Yin Fire	Ox	June	55	11: 23
July 7– August 8	Yin Fire	Sheep	Yin Fire	Ox	July	25	21: 46
August 8– September 8	Yang Earth	Monkey	Yin Fire	Ox	Aug	56	7: 26
September 8 – October 9	Yin Earth	Cock	Yin Fire	Ox	Sep	27	10: 00
October 9 – November 8	Yang Metal	Dog	Yin Fire	Ox	Oct	57	1: 11
November 8 – December 7	Yin Metal	Pig	Yin Fire	Ox	Nov	28	3: 46
December 7 – January 6	Yang Water	Rat	Yin Fire	Ox	Dec	58	20: 27

Branch	Pig	Rat	Ox	Tiger	Rabbit	Dragon	Snake	Horse	Sheep	Monkey	Cock	Dog
Main Element	Yang Water	Yin Water	Yin Earth	Yang Wood	Yin Wood	Yang Earth	Yang Fire	Yin Fire	Yin Earth	Yang Metal	Yin Metal	Yang Earth
Hidden Elements	Yang Wood		Yin Water Yin Metal	Yang Fire Yang Earth		Yin Wood Yin Water	Yang Earth Yang Metal	Yin Earth	Yin Fire Yin Wood	Yang Earth Yang Water		Yin Metal Yin Fire

1938

Find your Day Here	Month Stem	Month Branch	Year Stem	Year Branch	Day	Day	Time
January 6 – February 4	Yin Water	Ox	Yin Fire	Ox	Jan	29	7: 32
February 4— March 6	Yang Wood	Tiger	Yang Earth	Tiger	Feb	60	19:15
March 6— April 5	Yin Wood	Rabbit	Yang Earth	Tiger	Mar	28	13: 34
April 5— May 6	Yang Fire	Dragon	Yang Earth	Tiger	April	59	18: 49
May 6– June 6	Yin Fire	Snake	Yang Earth	Tiger	May	29	12: 36
June 6— July 8	Yang Earth	Horse	Yang Earth	Tiger	June	60	17: 07
July 8— August 8	Yin Earth	Sheep	Yang Earth	Tiger	July	30	3: 32
August 8— September 8	Yang Metal	Monkey	Yang Earth	Tiger	Aug	1	13: 13
September 8 – October 9	Yin Metal	Cock	Yang Earth	Tiger	Sep	32	15: 49
October 9— November 8	Yang Water	Dog	Yang Earth	Tiger	Oct	2	7: 02
November 8— December 8	Yin Water	Pig	Yang Earth	Tiger	Nov	33	9: 49
December 8 – January 6	Yang Wood	Rat	Yang Earth	Tiger	Dec	3	2: 23

1939

Find your Day Here	Month Stem	Month Branch	Year Stem	Year Branch	Day	Day	Time
January 6 – February 5	Yin Wood	Ox	Yang Earth	Tiger	Jan	34	13: 23
February 5— March 6	Yang Fire	Tiger	Yin Earth	Rabbit	Feb	5	1: 11
March 6 —April 6	Yin Fire	Rabbit	Yin Earth	Rabbit	Mar	33	19: 27
April 6— May 6	Yang Earth	Dragon	Yin Earth	Rabbit	April	4	: 38
May 6 – June 6	Yin Earth	Snake	Yin Earth	Rabbit	May	34	18: 21
June 6— July 8	Yang Metal	Horse	Yin Earth	Rabbit	June	5	22: 52
July 8— August 8	Yin Metal	Sheep	Yin Earth	Rabbit	July	35	9: 19
August 8— September 8	Yang Water	Monkey	Yin Earth	Rabbit	Aug	6	19: 04
September 8 – October 9	Yin Water	Cock	Yin Earth	Rabbit	Sep	37	21: 42
October 9— November 8	Yang Wood	Dog	Yin Earth	Rabbit	Oct	7	12: 57
November 8— December 8	Yin Wood	Pig	Yin Earth	Rabbit	Nov	38	15: 40
December 8 – January 6	Yang Fire	Rat	Yin Earth	Rabbit	Dec	8	8:18

Branch	Pig	Rat	Ox	Tiger	Rabbit	Dragon	Snake	Horse	Sheep	Monkey	Cock	Dog
Main Element	Yang Water	Yin Water	Yin Earth	Yang Wood	Yin Wood	Yang Earth	Yang Fire	Yin Fire	Yin Earth	Yang Metal	Yin Metal	Yang Earth
Hidden Elements	Yang Wood		Yin Water Yin Metal	Yang Fire Yang Earth		Yin Wood Yin Water	Yang Earth Yang Metal	Yin Earth	Yin Fire Yin Wood	Yang Earth Yang Water		Yin Metal Yin Fire

1940

	Month		Year				
Find your Day Here	Stem	Branch	Stem	Branch	Day	Day	Time
January 6 – February 5	Yin Fire	Ox	Yin Earth	Rabbit	Jan	39	19:24
February 5—29, March 6	Yang Earth	Tiger	Yang Metal	Dragon	Feb	10	7:08
March 6—April 5	Yin Earth	Rabbit	Yang Metal	Dragon	Mar	39	1:24
April 5 – May 6	Yang Metal	Dragon	Yang Metal	Dragon	April	10	6:35
May 6 – June 6	Yin Metal	Snake	Yang Metal	Dragon	May	40	:16
June 6 – July 7	Yang Water	Horse	Yang Metal	Dragon	June	11	4:44
July 7 – August 8	Yin Water	Sheep	Yang Metal	Dragon	July	41	15:08
August 8 – September 8	Yang Wood	Monkey	Yang Metal	Dragon	Aug	12	:52
September 8 – October 8	Yin Wood	Cock	Yang Metal	Dragon	Sep	43	3:30
October 8 – November 7	Yang Fire	Dog	Yang Metal	Dragon	Oct	13	18:43
November 7 – December 7	Yin Fire	Pig	Yang Metal	Dragon	Nov	44	21:27
December 7 – January 6	Yang Earth	Rat	Yang Metal	Dragon	Dec	14	13:58

1941

	Month		Year				
Find your Day Here	Stem	Branch	Stem	Branch	Day	Day	Time
January 6 – February 4	Yin Earth	Ox	Yang Metal	Dragon	Jan	45	1:04
February 4 – March 6	Yang Metal	Tiger	Yin Metal	Snake	Feb	16	12:50
March 6 – April 5	Yin Metal	Rabbit	Yin Metal	Snake	Mar	44	7:10
April 5 – May 6	Yang Water	Dragon	Yin Metal	Snake	April	15	12:25
May 6 – June 6	Yin Water	Snake	Yin Metal	Snake	May	45	6:10
June 6 – July 7	Yang Wood	Horse	Yin Metal	Snake	June	16	10:40
July 7 – August 8	Yin Wood	Sheep	Yin Metal	Snake	July	46	21:03
August 8 – September 8	Yang Fire	Monkey	Yin Metal	Snake	Aug	17	6:46
September 8 – October 9	Yin Fire	Cock	Yin Metal	Snake	Sep	48	9:24
October 9 – November 8	Yang Earth	Dog	Yin Metal	Snake	Oct	18	:39
November 8 – December 7	Yin Earth	Pig	Yin Metal	Snake	Nov	49	3:25
December 7 – January 6	Yang Metal	Rat	Yin Metal	Snake	Dec	19	19:57

Branch	Pig	Rat	Ox	Tiger	Rabbit	Dragon	Snake	Horse	Sheep	Monkey	Cock	Dog
Main Element	Yang Water	Yin Water	Yin Earth	Yang Wood	Yin Wood	Yang Earth	Yang Fire	Yin Fire	Yin Earth	Yang Metal	Yin Metal	Yang Earth
Hidden Elements	Yang Wood		Yin Water Yin Metal	Yang Fire Yang Earth		Yin Wood Yin Water	Yang Earth Yang Metal	Yin Earth	Yin Fire Yin Wood	Yang Earth Yang Water		Yin Metal Yin Fire

1942

Find your Day Here	Month Stem	Month Branch	Year Stem	Year Branch	Day	Day	Time
January 6 – February 4	Yin Metal	Ox	Yin Metal	Snake	Jan	50	7:03
February 4 – March 6	Yang Water	Tiger	Yang Water	Horse	Feb	21	18:49
March 6 – April 5	Yin Water	Rabbit	Yang Water	Horse	Mar	49	13:10
April 5 – May 6	Yang Wood	Dragon	Yang Water	Horse	April	20	18:24
May 6 – June 6	Yin Wood	Snake	Yang Water	Horse	May	50	12:07
June 6 – July 8	Yang Fire	Horse	Yang Water	Horse	June	21	16:37
July 8 – August 8	Yin Fire	Sheep	Yang Water	Horse	July	51	2:52
August 8 – September 8	Yang Earth	Monkey	Yang Water	Horse	Aug	22	12:31
September 8 – October 9	Yin Earth	Cock	Yang Water	Horse	Sep	53	15:07
October 9 – November 8	Yang Metal	Dog	Yang Water	Horse	Oct	23	6:22
November 8 – December 8	Yin Metal	Pig	Yang Water	Horse	Nov	54	9:12
December 8 – January 6	Yang Water	Rat	Yang Water	Horse	Dec	24	1:47

1943

Find your Day Here	Month Stem	Month Branch	Year Stem	Year Branch	Day	Day	Time
January 6 –February 5	Yin Water	Ox	Yang Water	Horse	Jan	55	12:55
February 5 – March 6	Yang Wood	Tiger	Yin Water	Sheep	Feb	26	: 40
March 6 – April 6	Yin Wood	Rabbit	Yin Water	Sheep	Mar	54	18: 59
April 6 – May 6	Yang Fire	Dragon	Yin Water	Sheep	April	25	: 12
May 6 – June 6	Yin Fire	Snake	Yin Water	Sheep	May	55	17:54
June 6 – July 8	Yang Earth	Horse	Yin Water	Sheep	June	26	22 19
July 8 – August 8	Yin Earth	Sheep	Yin Water	Sheep	July	56	8:39
August 8 – September 8	Yang Metal	Monkey	Yin Water	Sheep	Aug	27	18: 19
September 8 – October 9	Yin Metal	Cock	Yin Water	Sheep	Sep	58	20: 56
October 9 – November 8	Yang Water	Dog	Yin Water	Sheep	Oct	28	12: 11
November 8 – December 8	Yin Water	Pig	Yin Water	Sheep	Nov	59	14: 59
December 8 – January 6	Yang Wood	Rat	Yin Water	Sheep	Dec	29	7: 33

Branch	Pig	Rat	Ox	Tiger	Rabbit	Dragon	Snake	Horse	Sheep	Monkey	Cock	Dog
Main Element	Yang Water	Yin Water	Yin Earth	Yang Wood	Yin Wood	Yang Earth	Yang Fire	Yin Fire	Yin Earth	Yang Metal	Yin Metal	Yang Earth
Hidden Elements	Yang Wood		Yin Water Yin Metal	Yang Fire Yang Earth		Yin Wood Yin Water	Yang Earth Yang Metal	Yin Earth	Yin Fire Yin Wood	Yang Earth Yang Water		Yin Metal Yin Fire

1944

Find your Day Here	Month Stem	Month Branch	Year Stem	Year Branch	Day	Day	Time
January 6 – February 5	Yin Wood	Ox	Yin Water	Sheep	Jan	60	18: 40
February 5-29, March 6	Yang Fire	Tiger	Yang Wood	Monkey	Feb	31	6: 23
March 6—April 5	Yin Fire	Rabbit	Yang Wood	Monkey	Mar	60	: 41
April 5—May 6	Yang Earth	Dragon	Yang Wood	Monkey	April	31	5: 54
May 5—June 6	Yin Earth	Snake	Yang Wood	Monkey	May	1	23: 40
June 6—July 7	Yang Metal	Horse	Yang Wood	Monkey	June	32	4: 11
July 7—August 8	Yin Metal	Sheep	Yang Wood	Monkey	July	2	14: 37
August 8— September 8	Yang Water	Monkey	Yang Wood	Monkey	Aug	33	: 19
September 8—October 8	Yin Water	Cock	Yang Wood	Monkey	Sep	4	2:56
October 8— November 7	Yang Wood	Dog	Yang Wood	Monkey	Oct	34	18:09
November 7— December 7	Yin Wood	Pig	Yang Wood	Monkey	Nov	5	20: 55
December 7—January 6	Yang Fire	Rat	Yang Wood	Monkey	Dec	35	13: 28

1945

Find your Day Here	Month Stem	Month Branch	Year Stem	Year Branch	Day	Day	Time
January 6 – February 4	Yin Fire	Ox	Yang Wood	Monkey	Jan	6	:35
February 4— March 6	Yang Earth	Tiger	Yin Wood	Cock	Feb	37	12:20
March 6—April 5	Yin Earth	Rabbit	Yin Wood	Cock	Mar	5	6:38
April 5— May 6	Yang Metal	Dragon	Yin Wood	Cock	April	36	11:52
May 6 – June 6	Yin Metal	Snake	Yin Wood	Cock	May	6	5:37
June 6 – July 7	Yang Water	Horse	Yin Wood	Cock	June	37	10:06
July 7— August 8	Yin Water	Sheep	Yin Wood	Cock	July	7	20:27
August 8—September 8	Yang Wood	Monkey	Yin Wood	Cock	Aug	38	6:06
September 8— October 8	Yin Wood	Cock	Yin Wood	Cock	Sep	9	8:39
October 8— November 8	Yang Fire	Dog	Yin Wood	Cock	Oct	39	23:50
November 8—December 7	Yin Fire	Pig	Yin Wood	Cock	Nov	10	2:35
December 7— January 6	Yang Earth	Rat	Yin Wood	Cock	Dec	40	19:08

Branch	Pig	Rat	Ox	Tiger	Rabbit	Dragon	Snake	Horse	Sheep	Monkey	Cock	Dog
Main Element	Yang Water	Yin Water	Yin Earth	Yang Wood	Yin Wood	Yang Earth	Yang Fire	Yin Fire	Yin Earth	Yang Metal	Yin Metal	Yang Earth
Hidden Elements	Yang Wood		Yin Water Yin Metal	Yang Fire Yang Earth		Yin Wood Yin Water	Yang Earth Yang Metal	Yin Earth	Yin Fire Yin Wood	Yang Earth Yang Water		Yin Metal Yin Fire

1946

Find your Day Here	Month Stem	Month Branch	Year Stem	Year Branch	Day	Day	Time
January 6 – February 4	Yin Earth	Ox	Yin Wood	Cock	Jan	11	6:17
February 4— March 6	Yang Metal	Tiger	Yang Fire	Dog	Feb	42	18:04
March 6—April 5	Yin Metal	Rabbit	Yang Fire	Dog	Mar	10	12:25
April 5— May 6	Yang Water	Dragon	Yang Fire	Dog	April	41	17:39
May 6 – June 6	Yin Water	Snake	Yang Fire	Dog	May	11	11:22
June 6 – July 8	Yang Wood	Horse	Yang Fire	Dog	June	42	15:49
July 8— August 8	Yin Wood	Sheep	Yang Fire	Dog	July	12	2:11
August 8—September 8	Yang Fire	Monkey	Yang Fire	Dog	Aug	43	11:52
September 8— October 9	Yin Fire	Cock	Yang Fire	Dog	Sep	14	14:28
October 9— November 8	Yang Earth	Dog	Yang Fire	Dog	Oct	44	5:42
November 8—December 8	Yin Earth	Pig	Yang Fire	Dog	Nov	15	8:28
December 8— January 6	Yang Metal	Rat	Yang Fire	Dog	Dec	45	1:01

1947

Find your Day Here	Month Stem	Month Branch	Year Stem	Year Branch	Day	Day	Time
January 6 – February 5	Yin Metal	Ox	Yang Fire	Dog	Jan	16	12:11
February 4 - March 6	Yang Water	Tiger	Yin Fire	Pig	Feb	47	23:55
March 6—April 5	Yin Water	Rabbit	Yin Fire	Pig	Mar	15	18:12
April 5—May 6	Yang Wood	Dragon	Yin Fire	Pig	April	46	23:23
May 6—June 6	Yin Wood	Snake	Yin Fire	Pig	May	16	17:05
June 6—July 8	Yang Fire	Horse	Yin Fire	Pig	June	47	21:33
July 8—August 8	Yin Fire	Sheep	Yin Fire	Pig	July	17	7:56
August 8—September 8	Yang Earth	Monkey	Yin Fire	Pig	Aug	48	17:39
September 8—October 9	Yin Earth	Cock	Yin Fire	Pig	Sep	19	21:07
October 9—November 8	Yang Metal	Dog	Yin Fire	Pig	Oct	49	11:32
November 8 - December 8	Yin Metal	Pig	Yin Fire	Pig	Nov	20	14:19
December 8—January 6	Yang Water	Rat	Yin Fire	Pig	Dec	50	6:53

Branch	Pig	Rat	Ox	Tiger	Rabbit	Dragon	Snake	Horse	Sheep	Monkey	Cock	Dog
Main Element	Yang Water	Yin Water	Yin Earth	Yang Wood	Yin Wood	Yang Earth	Yang Fire	Yin Fire	Yin Earth	Yang Metal	Yin Metal	Yang Earth
Hidden Elements	Yang Wood		Yin Water Yin Metal	Yang Fire Yang Earth		Yin Wood Yin Water	Yang Earth Yang Metal	Yin Earth	Yin Fire Yin Wood	Yang Earth Yang Water		Yin Metal Yin Fire

1948

Find your Day Here	Month Stem	Month Branch	Year Stem	Year Branch	Day	Day	Time
January 6 – February 5	Yin Water	Ox	Yin Fire	Pig	Jan	21	18:01
February 5—29, March 5	Yang Wood	Tiger	Yang Earth	Rat	Feb	52	5:42
March 5—April 5	Yin Wood	Rabbit	Yang Earth	Rat	Mar	21	23:58
April 5—May 5	Yang Fire	Dragon	Yang Earth	Rat	April	52	5:10
May 5—June 6	Yin Fire	Snake	Yang Earth	Rat	May	22	22:53
June 6—July 7	Yang Earth	Horse	Yang Earth	Rat	June	53	3:21
July 7—August 7	Yin Earth	Sheep	Yang Earth	Rat	July	23	13:44
August 7—September 8	Yang Metal	Monkey	Yang Earth	Rat	Aug	54	23:27
September 8—October 8	Yin Metal	Cock	Yang Earth	Rat	Sep	25	2:06
October 8—November 7	Yang Water	Dog	Yang Earth	Rat	Oct	55	17:21
November 7—December 7	Yin Water	Pig	Yang Earth	Rat	Nov	26	20:07
December 7—January 6	Yang Wood	Rat	Yang Earth	Rat	Dec	56	12:38

1949

Find your Day Here	Month Stem	Month Branch	Year Stem	Year Branch	Day	Day	Time
January 6 – February 4	Yin Wood	Ox	Yang Earth	Rat	Jan	27	23:42
February 4—March 6	Yang Fire	Tiger	Yin Earth	Ox	Feb	58	11:23
March 6—April 5	Yin Fire	Rabbit	Yin Earth	Ox	Mar	26	5:40
April 5—May 6	Yang Earth	Dragon	Yin Earth	Ox	April	57	10:52
May 6—June 6	Yin Earth	Snake	Yin Earth	Ox	May	27	4:37
June 6—July 7	Yang Metal	Horse	Yin Earth	Ox	June	58	9:07
July 7—August 8	Yin Metal	Sheep	Yin Earth	Ox	July	28	19:32
August 8—September 8	Yang Water	Monkey	Yin Earth	Ox	Aug	59	5:16
September 8—October 8	Yin Water	Cock	Yin Earth	Ox	Sep	30	7:55
October 8 – November 8	Yang Wood	Dog	Yin Earth	Ox	Oct	60	23:12
November 8 – December 7	Yin Wood	Pig	Yin Earth	Ox	Nov	31	2:00
December 7 – January 6	Yang Fire	Rat	Yin Earth	Ox	Dec	1	18:34

Branch	Pig	Rat	Ox	Tiger	Rabbit	Dragon	Snake	Horse	Sheep	Monkey	Cock	Dog
Main Element	Yang Water	Yin Water	Yin Earth	Yang Wood	Yin Wood	Yang Earth	Yang Fire	Yin Fire	Yin Earth	Yang Metal	Yin Metal	Yang Earth
Hidden Elements	Yang Wood		Yin Water Yin Metal	Yang Fire Yang Earth		Yin Wood Yin Water	Yang Earth Yang Metal	Yin Earth	Yin Fire Yin Wood	Yang Earth Yang Water		Yin Metal Yin Fire

1950

Find your Day Here	Month Stem	Month Branch	Year Stem	Year Branch	Day	Day	Time
January 6- February 4	Yin Fire	Ox	Yin Earth	Ox	Jan	32	5: 39
February 4 – March 6	Yang Earth	Tiger	Yang Metal	Tiger	Feb	3	17: 21
March 6 – April 5	Yin Earth	Rabbit	Yang Metal	Tiger	Mar	31	11: 36
April 5 – May 6	Yang Metal	Dragon	Yang Metal	Tiger	April	2	16: 45
May 6 – June 6	Yin Metal	Snake	Yang Metal	Tiger	May	32	10: 25
June 6 – July 8	Yang Water	Horse	Yang Metal	Tiger	June	3	14: 52
July 8 – August 8	Yin Water	Sheep	Yang Metal	Tiger	July	33	1: 14
August 8 – September 8	Yang Wood	Monkey	Yang Metal	Tiger	Aug	4	10:56
September 8 – October 9	Yin Wood	Cock	Yang Metal	Tiger	Sep	35	13: 34
October 9 – November 8	Yang Fire	Dog	Yang Metal	Tiger	Oct	5	4:52
November 8 – December 8	Yin Fire	Pig	Yang Metal	Tiger	Nov	36	7: 44
December 8 – January 6	Yang Earth	Rat	Yang Metal	Tiger	Dec	6	: 22

1951

Find your Day Here	Month Stem	Month Branch	Year Stem	Year Branch	Day	Day	Time
January 6- February 4	Yin Earth	Ox	Yang Metal	Tiger	Jan	37	11:31
February 4 – March 7	Yang Metal	Tiger	Yin Metal	Rabbit	Feb	8	23:14
March 7 – April 5	Yin Metal	Rabbit	Yin Metal	Rabbit	Mar	36	17:27
April 6 – May 7	Yang Water	Dragon	Yin Metal	Rabbit	April	7	22:33
May 7 – June 7	Yin Water	Snake	Yin Metal	Rabbit	May	37	16:10
June 7 – July 8	Yang Wood	Horse	Yin Metal	Rabbit	June	8	20:33
July 8 – August 8	Yin Wood	Sheep	Yin Metal	Rabbi t	July	38	6:54
August 8 – September 8	Yang Fire	Monkey	Yin Metal	Rabbit	Aug	9	16:38
September 8 – October 9	Yin Fire	Cock	Yin Metal	Rabbit	Sep	40	19:19
October 9 – November 8	Yang Earth	Dog	Yin Metal	Rabbit	Oct	10	10:37
November 8 – December 8	Yin Earth	Pig	Yin Metal	Rabbit	Nov	41	13:27
December 8 – January 6	Yang Metal	Rat	Yin Metal	Rabbit	Dec	11	6:03

Branch	Pig	Rat	Ox	Tiger	Rabbit	Dragon	Snake	Horse	Sheep	Monkey	Cock	Dog
Main Element	Yang Water	Yin Water	Yin Earth	Yang Wood	Yin Wood	Yang Earth	Yang Fire	Yin Fire	Yin Earth	Yang Metal	Yin Metal	Yang Earth
Hidden Elements	Yang Wood		Yin Water Yin Metal	Yang Fire Yang Earth		Yin Wood Yin Water	Yang Earth Yang Metal	Yin Earth	Yin Fire Yin Wood	Yang Earth Yang Water		Yin Metal Yin Fire

1952

Find your Day Here	Month Stem	Month Branch	Year Stem	Year Branch	Day	Day	Time
January 6- February 5	Yin Metal	Ox	Yin Metal	Rabbit	Jan	42	17:10
February 5 – 29, March 5	Yang Water	Tiger	Yang Water	Dragon	Feb	13	4:53
March 5 – April 5	Yin Water	Rabbit	Yang Water	Dragon	Mar	42	23:08
April 5 – May 5	Yang Wood	Dragon	Yang Water	Dragon	April	13	4:16
May 5 – June 6	Yin Wood	Snake	Yang Water	Dragon	May	43	21:54
June 6 – July 7	Yang Fire	Horse	Yang Water	Dragon	June	14	2:21
July 7 – August 7	Yin Fire	She ep	Yang Water	Dragon	July	44	12:45
August 7 – September 8	Yang Earth	Monkey	Yang Water	Dragon	Aug	15	22:32
September 8 – October 8	Yin Earth	Cock	Yang Water	Dragon	Sep	46	1:14
October 8 – November 7	Yang Metal	Dog	Yang Water	Dragon	Oct	16	16:33
November 7 – December 7	Yin Metal	Pig	Yang Water	Dragon	Nov	47	19:22
December 7 – January 5	Yang Water	Rat	Yang Water	Dragon	Dec	17	11:56

1953

Find your Day Here	Month Stem	Month Branch	Year Stem	Year Branch	Day	Day	Time
January 5- February 4	Yin Water	Ox	Yang Water	Dragon	Jan	48	23: 03
February 4 – March 6	Yang Wood	Tiger	Yin Water	Snake	Feb	19	10: 46
March 6 – April 5	Yin Wood	Rabbit	Yin Water	Snake	Mar	47	5:03
April 5 – May 6	Yang Fire	Dragon	Yin Water	Snake	April	18	10:13
May 6 – June 6	Yin Fire	Snake	Yin Water	Snake	May	48	3:53
June 6 – July 7	Yang Earth	Horse	Yin Water	Snake	June	19	8:17
July 7 – August 8	Yin Earth	Sheep	Yin Water	Snake	July	49	18:36
August 8 – September 8	Yang Metal	Monkey	Yin Water	Snake	Aug	20	4:15
September 8 – October 8	Yin Metal	Cock	Yin Water	Snake	Sep	51	6:54
October 8 – November 8	Yang Water	Dog	Yin Water	Snake	Oct	21	22:11
November 8 – December 7	Yin Water	Pig	Yin Water	Snake	Nov	52	1:02
December 7 – January 6	Yang Wood	Rat	Yin Water	Snake	Dec	22	17:38

Branch	Pig	Rat	Ox	Tiger	Rabbit	Dragon	Snake	Horse	Sheep	Monkey	Cock	Dog
Main Element	Yang Water	Yin Water	Yin Earth	Yang Wood	Yin Wood	Yang Earth	Yang Fire	Yin Fire	Yin Earth	Yang Metal	Yin Metal	Yang Earth
Hidden Elements	Yang Wood		Yin Water Yin Metal	Yang Fire Yang Earth		Yin Wood Yin Water	Yang Earth Yang Metal	Yin Earth	Yin Fire Yin Wood	Yang Earth Yang Water		Yin Metal Yin Fire

1954

	Month		Year				
Find your Day Here	Stem	Branch	Stem	Branch	Day	Day	Time
January 6- February 4	Yin Wood	Ox	Yin Water	Snake	Jan	53	4:46
February 4 – March 6	Yang Fire	Tiger	Yang Wood	Horse	Feb	24	16:31
March 6 – April 5	Yin Fire	Rabbit	Yang Wood	Horse	Mar	52	10:49
April 5 – May 6	Yang Earth	Dragon	Yang Wood	Horse	April	23	16:00
May 6 – June 6	Yin Earth	Snake	Yang Wood	Horse	May	53	9:39
June 6 – July 8	Yang Metal	Horse	Yang Wood	Horse	June	24	14:02
July 8 – August 8	Yin Metal	Shee p	Yang Wood	Horse	July	54	:20
August 8 – September 8	Yang Water	Monkey	Yang Wood	Horse	Aug	25	10:00
September 8 – October 9	Yin Water	Cock	Yang Wood	Horse	Sep	56	12:39
October 9 – November 8	Yang Wood	Dog	Yang Wood	Horse	Oct	26	3:58
November 8 – December 7	Yin Wood	Pig	Yang Wood	Horse	Nov	57	6:51
December 7 – January 6	Yang Fire	Rat	Yang Wood	Horse	Dec	27	23:29

1955

	Month		Year				
Find your Day Here	Stem	Branch	Stem	Branch	Day	Day	Time
January 6- February 4	Yin Fire	Ox	Yang Wood	Horse	Jan	58	10: 36
February 4 – March 6	Yang Earth	Tiger	Yin Wood	Sheep	Feb	29	22: 18
March 6 – April 5	Yin Earth	Rabbit	Yin Wood	Sheep	Mar	57	16: 32
April 5 – May 6	Yang Metal	Dragon	Yin Wood	Sheep	April	28	21: 39
May 6 – June 6	Yin Metal	Snake	Yin Wood	Sheep	May	58	15: 18
June 6 – July 8	Yang Water	Horse	Yin Wood	Sheep	June	29	19: 44
July 8 – August 8	Yin Water	Sheep	Yin Wood	Sheep	July	59	6: 07
August 8 – September 8	Yang Wood	Monkey	Yin Wood	Sheep	Aug	30	15: 50
September 8 – October 9	Yin Wood	Cock	Yin Wood	Sheep	Sep	1	18: 32
October 9 – November 8	Yang Fire	Dog	Yin Wood	Sheep	Oct	31	9: 53
November 8 – December 8	Yin Fire	Pig	Yin Wood	Sheep	Nov	2	12: 46
December 8 – January 6	Yang Earth	Rat	Yin Wood	Sheep	Dec	32	5: 23

Branch	Pig	Rat	Ox	Tiger	Rabbit	Dragon	Snake	Horse	Sheep	Monkey	Cock	Dog
Main Element	Yang Water	Yin Water	Yin Earth	Yang Wood	Yin Wood	Yang Earth	Yang Fire	Yin Fire	Yin Earth	Yang Metal	Yin Metal	Yang Earth
Hidden Elements	Yang Wood		Yin Water Yin Metal	Yang Fire Yang Earth		Yin Wood Yin Water	Yang Earth Yang Metal	Yin Earth	Yin Fire Yin Wood	Yang Earth Yang Water		Yin Metal Yin Fire

1956

Find your Day Here	Month Stem	Month Branch	Year Stem	Year Branch	Day	Day	Time
January 6 – February 5	Yin Earth	Ox	Yin Wood	Sheep	Jan	3	16: 31
February 5 – 29, March 5	Yang Metal	Tiger	Yang Fire	Monkey	Feb	34	4: 12
March 5 – April 5	Yin Metal	Rabbit	Yang Fire	Monkey	Mar	3	22: 25
April 5 – May 5	Yang Water	Dragon	Yang Fire	Monkey	April	34	3: 32
May 5 – June 6	Yin Water	Snake	Yang Fire	Monkey	May	4	21: 11
June 6 – July 7	Yang Wood	Horse	Yang Fire	Monkey	June	35	1: 36
July 7 – August 7	Yin Wood	Sheep	Yang Fire	Monkey	July	5	11: 59
August 7 – September 8	Yang Fire	Monkey	Yang Fire	Monkey	Aug	36	9: 41
September 8 – October 8	Yin Fire	Cock	Yang Fire	Monkey	Sep	7	: 20
October 8 – November 7	Yang Earth	Dog	Yang Fire	Monkey	Oct	37	15: 37
November 7 – December 7	Yin Earth	Pig	Yang Fire	Monkey	Nov	8	18: 27
December 7 – January 5	Yang Metal	Rat	Yang Fire	Monkey	Dec	38	11: 03

1957

Find your Day Here	Month Stem	Month Branch	Year Stem	Year Branch	Day	Day	Time
January 5 – February 4	Yin Metal	Ox	Yang Fire	Monkey	Jan	4	22: 11
February 4— March 6	Yang Water	Tiger	Yin Fire	Cock	Feb	40	9: 55
March 6— April 5	Yin Water	Rabbit	Yin Fire	Cock	Mar	8	4: 11
April 5— May 6	Yang Wood	Dragon	Yin Fire	Cock	April	39	9: 19
May 6—June 6	Yin Wood	Snake	Yin Fire	Cock	May	9	2: 59
June 6— July 7	Yang Fire	Horse	Yin Fire	Cock	June	40	7: 25
July 7— August 8	Yin Fire	Sheep	Yin Fire	Cock	July	10	17: 49
August 8— September 8	Yang Earth	Monkey	Yin Fire	Cock	Aug	41	3: 33
September 8—October 8	Yin Earth	Cock	Yin Fire	Cock	Sep	12	6: 13
October 8— November 7	Yang Metal	Dog	Yin Fire	Cock	Oct	42	21: 31
November 7— December 7	Yin Metal	Pig	Yin Fire	Cock	Nov	13	12: 21
December 7—January 6	Yang Water	Rat	Yin Fire	Cock	Dec	43	16:57

Branch	Pig	Rat	Ox	Tiger	Rabbit	Dragon	Snake	Horse	Sheep	Monkey	Cock	Dog
Main Element	Yang Water	Yin Water	Yin Earth	Yang Wood	Yin Wood	Yang Earth	Yang Fire	Yin Fire	Yin Earth	Yang Metal	Yin Metal	Yang Earth
Hidden Elements	Yang Wood		Yin Water Yin Metal	Yang Fire Yang Earth		Yin Wood Yin Water	Yang Earth Yang Metal	Yin Earth	Yin Fire Yin Wood	Yang Earth Yang Water		Yin Metal Yin Fire

1958

	Month		Year				
Find your Day Here	Stem	Branch	Stem	Branch	Day	Day	Time
January 6—February 4	Yin Water	Ox	Yin Fire	Cock	Jan	14	4: 05
February 4 – March 6	Yang Wood	Tiger	Yang Earth	Dog	Feb	45	15: 49
March 6 – April 5	Yin Wood	Rabbit	Yang Earth	Dog	Mar	13	10: 06
April 5 – May 6	Yang Fire	Dragon	Yang Earth	Dog	April	44	15: 13
May 6 – June 6	Yin Fire	Snake	Yang Earth	Dog	May	14	8: 50
June 6 – July 8	Yang Earth	Horse	Yang Earth	Dog	June	45	13: 13
July 8 – August 8	Yin Earth	Sheep	Yang Earth	Dog	July	15	23: 34
August 8 – September 8	Yang Metal	Monkey	Yang Earth	Dog	Aug	46	9: 18
September 8 – October 9	Yin Metal	Cock	Yang Earth	Dog	Sep	17	12: 00
October 9 – November 8	Yang Water	Dog	Yang Earth	Dog	Oct	47	3: 20
November 8 – December 7	Yin Water	Pig	Yang Earth	Dog	Nov	18	6: 13
December 7 – January 6	Yang Wood	Rat	Yang Earth	Dog	Dec	48	22: 50

1959

	Month		Year				
Find your Day Here	Stem	Branch	Stem	Branch	Day	Day	Time
January 6 – February 4	Yin Wood	Ox	Yang Earth	Dog	Jan	19	9: 59
February 4— March 6	Yang Fire	Tiger	Yin Earth	Pig	Feb	50	21: 42
March 6— April 5	Yin Fire	Rabbit	Yin Earth	Pig	Mar	18	15: 57
April 5— May 6	Yang Earth	Dragon	Yin Earth	Pig	April	49	21: 04
May 6 – June 6	Yin Earth	Snake	Yin Earth	Pig	May	19	14: 39
June 6— July 8	Yang Metal	Horse	Yin Earth	Pig	June	50	19: 01
July 8— August 8	Yin Metal	Sh eep	Yin Earth	Pig	July	20	5: 21
August 8— September 8	Yang Water	Monkey	Yin Earth	Pig	Aug	51	15: 05
September 8—October 8	Yin Water	Cock	Yin Earth	Pig	Sep	22	17: 49
October 9— November 8	Yang Wood	Dog	Yin Earth	Pig	Oct	52	9: 11
November 8— December 8	Yin Wood	Pig	Yin Earth	Pig	Nov	23	12: 03
December 8—January 6	Yang Fire	Rat	Yin Earth	Pig	Dec	53	4: 38

Branch	Pig	Rat	Ox	Tiger	Rabbit	Dragon	Snake	Horse	Sheep	Monkey	Cock	Dog
Main Element	Yang Water	Yin Water	Yin Earth	Yang Wood	Yin Wood	Yang Earth	Yang Fire	Yin Fire	Yin Earth	Yang Metal	Yin Metal	Yang Earth
Hidden Elements	Yang Wood		Yin Water Yin Metal	Yang Fire Yang Earth		Yin Wood Yin Water	Yang Earth Yang Metal	Yin Earth	Yin Fire Yin Wood	Yang Earth Yang Water		Yin Metal Yin Fire

1960

Find your Day Here	Month Stem	Month Branch	Year Stem	Year Branch	Day	Day	Time
January 6 – February 5	Yin Fire	Ox	Yin Earth	Pig	Jan	24	15: 43
February 5 –29, March 5	Yang Earth	Tiger	Yang Metal	Rat	Feb	55	3: 24
March 5— April 5	Yin Earth	Rabbit	Yang Metal	Rat	Mar	24	21: 36
April 5— May 5	Yang Metal	Dragon	Yang Metal	Rat	April	55	2: 44
May 5—June 6	Yin Metal	Snake	Yang Metal	Rat	May	25	20: 23
June 6— July 7	Yang Water	Horse	Yang Metal	Rat	June	56	: 49
July 7— August 7	Yin Water	S heep	Yang Metal	Rat	July	26	11: 13
August 7— September 7	Yang Wood	Monkey	Yang Metal	Rat	Aug	57	21: 00
September 7—October 8	Yin Wood	Cock	Yang Metal	Rat	Sep	28	23: 46
October 8— November 7	Yang Fire	Dog	Yang Metal	Rat	Oct	58	15: 09
November 7— December 7	Yin Fire	Pig	Yang Metal	Rat	Nov	29	18: 02
December 7—January 5	Yang Earth	Rat	Yang Metal	Rat	Dec	59	10:38

1961

Find your Day Here	Month Stem	Month Branch	Year Stem	Year Branch	Day	Day	Time
January 5 – February 4	Yin Earth	Ox	Yang Metal	Rat	Jan	30	21: 43
February 4— March 6	Yang Metal	Tiger	Yin Metal	Ox	Feb	1	9: 22
March 6— April 5	Yin Metal	Rabbit	Yin Metal	Ox	Mar	29	3: 35
April 5— May 6	Yang Water	Dragon	Yin Metal	Ox	April	60	8: 42
May 6—June 6	Yin Water	Snake	Yin Metal	Ox	May	30	2: 21
June 6— July 7	Yang Wood	Horse	Yin Metal	Ox	June	1	6: 46
July 7— August 8	Yin Wood	S heep	Yin Metal	Ox	July	31	17: 07
August 8— September 8	Yang Fire	Monkey	Yin Metal	Ox	Aug	2	2: 49
September 8—October 8	Yin Fire	Cock	Yin Metal	Ox	Sep	33	5: 29
October 8— November 7	Yang Earth	Dog	Yin Metal	Ox	Oct	3	20: 51
November 7— December 7	Yin Earth	Pig	Yin Metal	Ox	Nov	34	23: 46
December 7—January 6	Yang Metal	Rat	Yin Metal	Ox	Dec	4	16: 26

Branch	Pig	Rat	Ox	Tiger	Rabbit	Dragon	Snake	Horse	Sheep	Monkey	Cock	Dog
Main Element	Yang Water	Yin Water	Yin Earth	Yang Wood	Yin Wood	Yang Earth	Yang Fire	Yin Fire	Yin Earth	Yang Metal	Yin Metal	Yang Earth
Hidden Elements	Yang Wood		Yin Water Yin Metal	Yang Fire Yang Earth		Yin Wood Yin Water	Yang Earth Yang Metal	Yin Earth	Yin Fire Yin Wood	Yang Earth Yang Water		Yin Metal Yin Fire

1962

Find your Day Here	Month Stem	Month Branch	Year Stem	Year Branch	Day	Day	Time
January 6 – February 4	Yin Metal	Ox	Yin Metal	Ox	Jan	35	3: 35
February 4— March 6	Yang Water	Tiger	Yang Water	Tiger	Feb	6	15: 18
March 6— April 5	Yin Water	Rabbit	Yang Water	Tiger	Mar	6	9: 30
April 5— May 6	Yang Wood	Dragon	Yang Water	Tiger	April	6	14: 34
May 6 – June 6	Yin Wood	Snake	Yang Water	Tiger	May	35	8: 10
June 6— July 7	Yang Fire	Horse	Yang Water	Tiger	June	6	12: 31
July 7— August 8	Yin Fire	Sheep	Yang Water	Tig er	July	36	22: 51
August 8— September 8	Yang Earth	Monkey	Yang Water	Tiger	Aug	7	8: 34
September 8—October 9	Yin Earth	Cock	Yang Water	Tiger	Sep	38	11: 16
October 9— November 8	Yang Metal	Dog	Yang Water	Tiger	Oct	8	2: 38
November 8— December 7	Yin Metal	Pig	Yang Water	Tiger	Nov	39	5: 35
December 7—January 6	Yang Water	Rat	Yang Water	Tiger	Dec	9	22: 17

1963

Find your Day Here	Month Stem	Month Branch	Year Stem	Year Branch	Day	Day	Time
January 6 – February 4	Yin Water	Ox	Yang Water	Tiger	Jan	40	9: 27
February 4— March 6	Yang Wood	Tiger	Yin Water	Rabbit	Feb	11	21: 08
March 6— April 5	Yin Wood	Rabbit	Yin Water	Rabbit	Mar	39	15: 17
April 5— May 6	Yang Fire	Dragon	Yin Water	Rabbit	April	10	20: 19
May 6 – June 6	Yin Fire	Snake	Yin Water	Rabbit	May	40	13: 52
June 6— July 7	Yang Earth	Horse	Yin Water	Rabbit	June	11	18: 15
July 8— August 8	Yin Earth	Sheep	Yin Water	Rabbit	July	41	4: 38
August 8— September 8	Yang Metal	Monkey	Yin Water	Rabbit	Aug	12	14: 26
September 8 – October 9	Yin Metal	Cock	Yin Water	Rabbit	Sep	43	17: 12
October 9— November 8	Yang Water	Dog	Yin Water	Ra bbit	Oct	13	8: 36
November 8— December 8	Yin Water	Pig	Yin Water	Rabbit	Nov	44	11: 32
December 8—January 6	Yang Wood	Rat	Yin Water	Rabbit	Dec	14	4: 13

Branch	Pig	Rat	Ox	Tiger	Rabbit	Dragon	Snake	Horse	Sheep	Monkey	Cock	Dog
Main Element	Yang Water	Yin Water	Yin Earth	Yang Wood	Yin Wood	Yang Earth	Yang Fire	Yin Fire	Yin Earth	Yang Metal	Yin Metal	Yang Earth
Hidden Elements	Yang Wood		Yin Water Yin Metal	Yang Fire Yang Earth		Yin Wood Yin Water	Yang Earth Yang Metal	Yin Earth	Yin Fire Yin Wood	Yang Earth Yang Water		Yin Metal Yin Fire

1964

Find your Day Here	Month Stem	Month Branch	Year Stem	Year Branch	Day	Day	Time
January 6- February 5	Yin Wood	Ox	Yin Water	Rabbit	Jan	45	15: 22
February 5-29,— March 5	Yang Fire	Tiger	Yang Wood	Dragon	Feb	16	3: 05
March 5 – April 5	Yin Fire	Rabbit	Yang Wood	Dragon	Mar	45	21: 16
April 5 – May 5	Yang Earth	Dragon	Yang Wood	Dragon	April	16	2: 18
May 5 – June 6	Yin Earth	Snake	Yang Wood	Dragon	May	46	19: 51
June 6 – July 7	Yang Metal	Horse	Yang Wood	Dragon	June	17	: 12
July 7 – August 7	Yin Metal	Sheep	Yang Wood	Dragon	July	47	10: 32
August 7 – September 7	Yang Water	Monkey	Yang Wood	Dragon	Aug	18	20: 16
September 7 – October 8	Yin Water	Cock	Yang Wood	Dragon	Sep	49	23:00
October 8 – November 7	Yang Wood	Dog	Yang Wood	Dragon	Oct	19	14: 22
November 7 – December 7	Yin Wood	Pig	Yang Wood	Dragon	Nov	50	17: 15
December 7 – January 5	Yang Fire	Rat	Yang Wood	Dragon	Dec	20	9: 53

1965

Find your Day Here	Month Stem	Month Branch	Year Stem	Year Branch	Day	Day	Time
January 5 – February 4	Yin Fire	Ox	Yang Wood	Dragon	Jan	51	21: 02
February 4— March 6	Yang Earth	Tiger	Yin Wood	Snake	Feb	27	8: 46
March 6— April 5	Yin Earth	Rabbit	Yin Wood	Snake	Mar	50	3: 01
April 5— May 6	Yang Metal	Dragon	Yin Wood	Snake	April	21	8: 07
May 6—June 6	Yin Metal	Snake	Yin Wood	Snake	May	51	1: 42
June 6— July 7	Yang Water	Horse	Yin Wood	Snake	June	22	6: 02
July 7— August 8	Yin Water	Sheep	Yin Wood	Snak e	July	52	16: 22
August 8— September 8	Yang Wood	Monkey	Yin Wood	Snake	Aug	23	2: 05
September 8 – October 8	Yin Wood	Cock	Yin Wood	Snake	Sep	54	4: 48
October 8— November 7	Yang Fire	Dog	Yin Wood	Snake	Oct	24	20: 11
November 7— December 7	Yin Fire	Pig	Yin Wood	Snake	Nov	55	23: 07
December 7—January 5	Yang Earth	Rat	Yin Wood	Snake	Dec	25	15: 46

Branch	Pig	Rat	Ox	Tiger	Rabbit	Dragon	Snake	Horse	Sheep	Monkey	Cock	Dog
Main Element	Yang Water	Yin Water	Yin Earth	Yang Wood	Yin Wood	Yang Earth	Yang Fire	Yin Fire	Yin Earth	Yang Metal	Yin Metal	Yang Earth
Hidden Elements	Yang Wood		Yin Water Yin Metal	Yang Fire Yang Earth		Yin Wood Yin Water	Yang Earth Yang Metal	Yin Earth	Yin Fire Yin Wood	Yang Earth Yang Water		Yin Metal Yin Fire

1966

Find your Day Here	Month Stem	Month Branch	Year Stem	Year Branch	Day	Day	Time
January 5 – February 4	Yin Earth	Ox	Yin Wood	Snake	Jan	56	2: 55
February 4 – 29, March 6	Yang Metal	Tiger	Yang Fire	Horse	Feb	27	14: 38
March 6 – April 5	Yin Metal	Rabbit	Yang Fire	Horse	Mar	55	8: 51
April 5 – May 6	Yang Water	Dragon	Yang Fire	Horse	April	26	13: 57
May 6 – June 6	Yin Water	Snake	Yang Fire	Horse	May	56	7: 31
June 6 – July 7	Yang Wood	Horse	Yang Fire	Horse	June	27	11: 50
July 7 – August 8	Yin Wood	Sheep	Yang Fire	Horse	July	57	22: 07
August 8– September 8	Yang Fire	Monkey	Yang Fire	Horse	Aug	28	7: 49
September 8 – October 9	Yin Fire	Cock	Yang Fire	Horse	Sep	59	10: 32
October 9 – November 8	Yang Earth	Dog	Yang Fire	Horse	Oct	29	1: 57
November 8 – December 7	Yin Earth	Pig	Yang Fire	Horse	Nov	60	4: 56
December 7 – January 6	Yang Metal	Rat	Yang Fire	Horse	Dec	30	21: 38

1967

Find your Day Here	Month Stem	Month Branch	Year Stem	Year Branch	Day	Day	Time
January 6 – February 4	Yin Metal	Ox	Yang Fire	Horse	Jan	1	8: 48
February 4— March 6	Yang Water	Tiger	Yin Fire	Sheep	Feb	32	20: 31
March 6— April 5	Yin Water	Rabbit	Yin Fire	Sheep	Mar	60	14: 42
April 5— May 6	Yang Wood	Dragon	Yin Fire	Sheep	April	31	19: 45
May 6 – June 6	Yin Wood	Snake	Yin Fire	Sheep	May	1	13: 18
June 6— July 8	Yang Fire	Horse	Yin Fire	Sheep	June	32	17: 36
July 8— August 8	Yin Fire	Sheep	Yin Fire	Sheep	July	2	3: 54
August 8— September 8	Yang Earth	Monkey	Yin Fire	Sheep	Aug	33	13: 35
September 8 – October 9	Yin Earth	Cock	Yin Fire	Sheep	Sep	4	16: 18
October 9— November 8	Yang Metal	Dog	Yin Fire	Sheep	Oct	34	7: 42
November 8— December 8	Yin Metal	Pig	Yin Fire	Sheep	Nov	5	10: 38
December 8—January 6	Yang Water	Rat	Yin Fire	Sheep	Dec	35	3: 18

Branch	Pig	Rat	Ox	Tiger	Rabbit	Dragon	Snake	Horse	Sheep	Monkey	Cock	Dog
Main Element	Yang Water	Yin Water	Yin Earth	Yang Wood	Yin Wood	Yang Earth	Yang Fire	Yin Fire	Yin Earth	Yang Metal	Yin Metal	Yang Earth
Hidden Elements	Yang Wood		Yin Water Yin Metal	Yang Fire Yang Earth		Yin Wood Yin Water	Yang Earth Yang Metal	Yin Earth	Yin Fire Yin Wood	Yang Earth Yang Water		Yin Metal Yin Fire

1968

Find your Day Here	Month Stem	Month Branch	Year Stem	Year Branch	Day	Day	Time
January 6 – February 5	Yin Water	Ox	Yin Fire	Sheep	Jan	6	14: 26
February 5 – 29,— March 5	Yang Wood	Tiger	Yang Earth	Monkey	Feb	37	2: 08
March 5— April 5	Yin Wood	Rabbit	Yang Earth	Monkey	Mar	6	20: 18
April 5— May 5	Yang Fire	Dragon	Yang Earth	Monkey	April	37	1: 21
May 5 – June 5	Yin Fire	Snake	Yang Earth	Monkey	May	7	18: 56
June 5— July 7	Yang Earth	Horse	Yang Earth	Monkey	June	38	23: 19
July 7— August 7	Yin Earth	S heep	Yang Earth	Monkey	July	8	9: 42
August 7— September 7	Yang Metal	Monkey	Yang Earth	Monkey	Aug	39	19: 27
September 7 – October 8	Yin Metal	Cock	Yang Earth	Monkey	Sep	10	22: 12
October 8— November 7	Yang Water	Dog	Yang Earth	Monkey	Oct	40	13: 35
November 7— December 7	Yin Water	Pig	Yang Earth	Monkey	Nov	11	16: 29
December 7—January 5	Yang Wood	Rat	Yang Earth	Monkey	Dec	41	9: 09

1969

Find your Day Here	Month Stem	Month Branch	Year Stem	Year Branch	Day	Day	Time
January 5 – February 4	Yin Wood	Ox	Yang Earth	Monkey	Jan	12	20: 17
February 4— March 6	Yang Fire	Tiger	Yin Earth	Cock	Feb	43	7: 59
March 6— April 5	Yin Fire	Rabbit	Yin Earth	Cock	Mar	11	2: 11
April 5— May 6	Yang Earth	Dragon	Yin Earth	Cock	April	42	7: 15
May 6 – June 6	Yin Earth	Snake	Yin Earth	Cock	May	12	: 50
June 6— July 7	Yang Metal	Horse	Yin Earth	Cock	June	43	5: 12
July 7— August 8	Yin Metal	Sheep	Yin Earth	Cock	July	13	15: 32
August 8— September 8	Yang Water	Monkey	Yin Earth	Cock	Aug	44	1: 14
September 8 – October 8	Yin Water	Cock	Yin Earth	Cock	Sep	15	3: 56
October 8— November 7	Yang Wood	Dog	Yin Earth	Cock	Oct	45	19: 17
November 7— December 7	Yin Wood	Pig	Yin Earth	Cock	Nov	16	22: 12
December 7—January 6	Yang Fire	Rat	Yin Earth	Cock	Dec	46	14: 51

Branch	Pig	Rat	Ox	Tiger	Rabbit	Dragon	Snake	Horse	Sheep	Monkey	Cock	Dog
Main Element	Yang Water	Yin Water	Yin Earth	Yang Wood	Yin Wood	Yang Earth	Yang Fire	Yin Fire	Yin Earth	Yang Metal	Yin Metal	Yang Earth
Hidden Elements	Yang Wood		Yin Water Yin Metal	Yang Fire Yang Earth		Yin Wood Yin Water	Yang Earth Yang Metal	Yin Earth	Yin Fire Yin Wood	Yang Earth Yang Water		Yin Metal Yin Fire

1970

Find your Day	Month Stem	Month Branch	Year Stem	Year Branch	Day	Day	Time
January 6 – February 4	Yin Fire	Ox	Yin Earth	Cock	Jan	17	1:59
February 4— March 6	Yang Earth	Tiger	Yang Metal	Dog	Feb	48	13:46
March 6— April 5	Yin Earth	Rabbit	Yang Metal	Dog	Mar	16	7:51
April 5— May 6	Yang Metal	Dragon	Yang Metal	Dog	April	47	12:54
May 6 – June 6	Yin Metal	Snake	Yang Metal	Dog	May	17	6:28
June 6— July 7	Yang Water	Horse	Yang Metal	Dog	June	48	10:51
July 7— August 8	Yin Water	Sheep	Yang Metal	Dog	July	18	21:14
August 8— September 8	Yang Wood	Monkey	Yang Metal	Dog	Aug	49	6:58
September 8 – October 9	Yin Wood	Cock	Yang Metal	Dog	Sep	20	9:42
October 9— November 8	Yang Fire	Dog	Yang Metal	Dog	Oct	50	1:06
November 8— December 7	Yin Fire	Pig	Yang Metal	Dog	Nov	21	4:01
December 7—January 6	Yang Earth	Rat	Yang Metal	Dog	Dec	51	21:41

1971

Find your Day Here	Month Stem	Month Branch	Year Stem	Year Branc	Day	Day	Time
January 6 – February 4	Yin Earth	Ox	Yang Metal	Dog	Jan	22	7: 45
February 4 – 29, March 6	Yang Metal	Tiger	Yin Metal	Pig	Feb	53	19 :26
March 6 – April 5	Yin Metal	Rabbit	Yin Metal	Pig	Mar	21	13: 35
April 5 – May 6	Yang Water	Dragon	Yin Metal	Pig	April	52	18: 36
May 6 – June 6	Yin Water	Snake	Yin Metal	Pig	May	22	12: 08
June 6 – July 8	Yang Wood	Horse	Yin Metal	Pig	June	53	16: 29
July 8 – August 8	Yin Wood	Sheep	Yin Metal	Pig	July	23	2:51
August 8– September 8	Yang Fire	Monkey	Yin Metal	Pig	Aug	54	12: 40
September 8 – October 9	Yin Fire	Cock	Yin Metal	Pig	Sep	25	17: 30
October 9 – November 8	Yang Earth	Dog	Yin Metal	Pig	Oct	55	6: 59
November 8 – December 8	Yin Earth	Pig	Yin Metal	Pig	Nov	26	9:57
December 8 – January 6	Yang Metal	Rat	Yin Metal	Pig	Dec	56	2:36

Branch	Pig	Rat	Ox	Tiger	Rabbit	Dragon	Snake	Horse	Sheep	Monkey	Cock	Dog
Main Element	Yang Water	Yin Water	Yin Earth	Yang Wood	Yin Wood	Yang Earth	Yang Fire	Yin Fire	Yin Earth	Yang Metal	Yin Metal	Yang Earth
Hidden Elements	Yang Wood		Yin Water Yin Metal	Yang Fire Yang Earth		Yin Wood Yin Water	Yang Earth Yang Metal	Yin Earth	Yin Fire Yin Wood	Yang Earth Yang Water		Yin Metal Yin Fire

1972

Find your Day Here	Month Stem	Month Branch	Year Stem	Year Branch	Day	Day	Time
January 6 – February 5	Yin Metal	Ox	Yin Metal	Pig	Jan	27	13: 43
February 5—29,— March 5	Yang Water	Tiger	Yang Water	Rat	Feb	58	13: 20
March 5— April 5	Yin Water	Rabbit	Yang Water	Rat	Mar	27	19: 28
April 5— May 5	Yang Wood	Dragon	Yang Water	Rat	April	58	12: 29
May 5 – June 5	Yin Wood	Snake	Yang Water	Rat	May	59	18: 16
June 5— July 7	Yang Fire	Horse	Yang Water	Rat	June	59	22: 22
July 7— August 7	Yin Fire	She ep	Yang Water	Rat	July	29	8:43
August 7— September 7	Yang Earth	Monkey	Yang Water	Rat	Aug	31	18: 29
September 7 – October 8	Yin Earth	Cock	Yang Water	Rat	Sep	31	21: 15
October 8— November 7	Yang Metal	Dog	Yang Water	Rat	Oct	1	14: 42
November 7— December 7	Yin Metal	Pig	Yang Water	Rat	Nov	32	15: 40
December 7—January 5	Yang Water	Rat	Yang Water	Rat	Dec	2	8:19

1973

Find your Day Here	Month Stem	Month Branch	Year Stem	Year Branch	Day	Day	Time
January 5 – February 4	Yin Water	Ox	Yang Water	Rat	Jan	33	19: 26
February 4— March 6	Yang Wood	Tiger	Yin Water	Ox	Feb	4	7: 04
March 6— April 5	Yin Wood	Rabbit	Yin Water	Ox	Mar	32	1: 13
April 5— May 5	Yang Fire	Dragon	Yin Water	Ox	April	3	6: 14
May 5 – June 6	Yin Fire	Snake	Yin Water	Ox	May	33	23: 47
June 6— July 7	Yang Earth	Horse	Yin Water	Ox	June	4	4: 07
July 7— August 8	Yin Earth	Sheep	Yin Water	Ox	July	34	14: 28
August 8— September 8	Yang Metal	Monkey	Yin Water	Ox	Aug	5	:13
September 8 – October 8	Yin Metal	Cock	Yin Water	Ox	Sep	36	3: 00
October 8— November 7	Yang Water	Dog	Yin Water	Ox	Oct	6	18:27
November 7— December 7	Yin Water	Pig	Yin Water	Ox	Nov	37	21: 28
December 7 – January 6	Yang Wood	Rat	Yin Water	Ox	Dec	7	14 :11

Branch	Pig	Rat	Ox	Tiger	Rabbit	Dragon	Snake	Horse	Sheep	Monkey	Cock	Dog
Main Element	Yang Water	Yin Water	Yin Earth	Yang Wood	Yin Wood	Yang Earth	Yang Fire	Yin Fire	Yin Earth	Yang Metal	Yin Metal	Yang Earth
Hidden Elements	Yang Wood		Yin Water Yin Metal	Yang Fire Yang Earth		Yin Wood Yin Water	Yang Earth Yang Metal	Yin Earth	Yin Fire Yin Wood	Yang Earth Yang Water		Yin Metal Yin Fire

1974

Find your Day Here	Month Stem	Month Branch	Year Stem	Year Branch	Day	Day	Time
January 6 – February 4	Yin Wood	Ox	Yin Water	Ox	Jan	38	1: 20
February 4— March 6	Yang Fire	Tiger	Yang Wood	Tiger	Feb	9	13: 00
March 6— April 5	Yin Fire	Rabbit	Yang Wood	Tiger	Mar	37	7: 07
April 5— May 6	Yang Earth	Dragon	Yang Wood	Tiger	April	8	12: 05
May 6 – June 6	Yin Earth	Snake	Yang Wood	Tiger	May	38	5: 34
June 6— July 7	Yang Metal	Horse	Yang Wood	Tiger	June	9	9: 52
July 7— August 8	Yin Metal	Sheep	Yang Wood	Tiger	July	39	20: 13
August 8— September 8	Yang Water	Monkey	Yang Wood	Tiger	Aug	10	5: 57
September 8 – October 9	Yin Water	Cock	Yang Wood	Tiger	Sep	41	8:45
October 9— November 8	Yang Wood	Dog	Yang Wood	Tiger	Oct	11	: 15
November 8— December 7	Yin Wood	Pig	Yang Wood	Tiger	Nov	42	3: 18
December 7 – January 6	Yang Fire	Rat	Yang Wood	Tiger	Dec	12	20: 05

1975

Find your Day Here	Month Stem	Month Branch	Year Stem	Year Branch	Day	Day	Time
January 6 – February 4	Yin Fire	Ox	Yang Wood	Tiger	Jan	43	7:18
February 4 —March 6	Yang Earth	Tiger	Yin Wood	Rabbit	Feb	14	18: 59
March 6 – April 5	Yin Earth	Rabbit	Yin Wood	Rabbit	Mar	42	13: 06
April 5 – May 6	Yang Metal	Dragon	Yin Wood	Rabbit	April	13	18: 02
May 6 – June 6	Yin Metal	Snake	Yin Wood	Rabbit	May	43	11: 27
June 6 – July 8	Yang Water	Horse	Yin Wood	Rabbit	June	14	15: 42
July 8 – August 8	Yin Water	Sheep	Yin Wood	Rabbit	July	44	2: 00
August 8– September 8	Yang Wood	Monkey	Yin Wood	Rabbit	Aug	15	11: 45
September 8 – October 9	Yin Wood	Cock	Yin Wood	Rabbit	Sep	46	14:33
October 9 – November 8	Yang Fire	Dog	Yin Wood	Rabbit	Oct	16	6: 02
November 8 – December 8	Yin Fire	Pig	Yin Wood	Rabbit	Nov	47	9: 03
December 8 – January 6	Yang Earth	Rat	Yin Wood	Rabbit	Dec	17	1: 46

Branch	Pig	Rat	Ox	Tiger	Rabbit	Dragon	Snake	Horse	Sheep	Monkey	Cock	Dog
Main Element	Yang Water	Yin Water	Yin Earth	Yang Wood	Yin Wood	Yang Earth	Yang Fire	Yin Fire	Yin Earth	Yang Metal	Yin Metal	Yang Earth
Hidden Elements	Yang Wood		Yin Water Yin Metal	Yang Fire Yang Earth		Yin Wood Yin Water	Yang Earth Yang Metal	Yin Earth	Yin Fire Yin Wood	Yang Earth Yang Water		Yin Metal Yin Fire

1976

Find your Day Here	Month Stem	Month Branch	Year Stem	Year Branch	Day	Day	Time
January 6 – February 5	Yin Earth	Ox	Yin Wood	Rabbit	Jan	48	12: 58
February 5— 29,—March 5	Yang Metal	Tiger	Yang Fire	Dragon	Feb	19	: 40
March 5— April 4	Yin Metal	Rabbit	Yang Fire	Dragon	Mar	48	18: 48
April 4— May 5	Yang Water	Dragon	Yang Fire	Dragon	April	19	23: 47
May 5 – June 5	Yin Water	Snake	Yang Fire	Dragon	May	49	17: 15
June 5— July 7	Yang Wood	Horse	Yang Fire	Dragon	June	20	21: 31
July 7— August 7	Yin Wood	Sheep	Yang Fire	Dragon	July	50	7: 51
August 7— September 7	Yang Fire	Monkey	Yang Fire	Dragon	Aug	21	17: 39
September 7 – October 8	Yin Fire	Cock	Yang Fire	Dragon	Sep	52	20:28
October 8— November 7	Yang Earth	Dog	Yang Fire	Drag on	Oct	22	11: 58
November 7— December 7	Yin Earth	Pig	Yang Fire	Dragon	Nov	53	14: 59
December 7—January 5	Yang Metal	Rat	Yang Fire	Dragon	Dec	23	7: 41

1977

Find your Day Here	Month Stem	Month Branch	Year Stem	Year Branch	Day	Day	Time
January 5 – February 4	Yin Metal	Ox	Yang Fire	Dragon	Jan	54	18: 51
February 4— March 6	Yang Water	Tiger	Yin Fire	Snake	Feb	25	6: 34
March 6— April 5	Yin Water	Rabbit	Yin Fire	Snake	Mar	53	: 44
April 5— May 5	Yang Wood	Dragon	Yin Fire	Snake	April	24	5: 46
May 5 – June 6	Yin Wood	Snake	Yin Fire	Snake	May	54	23: 16
June 6— July 7	Yang Fire	Horse	Yin Fire	Snake	June	25	3: 32
July 7— August 7	Yin Fire	Sheep	Yin Fire	Snake	July	55	13: 48
August 7— September 8	Yang Earth	Monkey	Yin Fire	Snake	Aug	26	23: 30
September 8 – October 8	Yin Earth	Cock	Yin Fire	Snake	Sep	57	2: 16
October 8— November 7	Yang Metal	Dog	Yin Fire	Snake	Oct	27	17: 44
November 7— December 7	Yin Metal	Pig	Yin Fire	Snake	Nov	58	20: 46
December 7 – January 6	Yang Water	Rat	Yin Fire	Snake	Dec	28	13: 31

Branch	Pig	Rat	Ox	Tiger	Rabbit	Dragon	Snake	Horse	Sheep	Monkey	Cock	Dog
Main Element	Yang Water	Yin Water	Yin Earth	Yang Wood	Yin Wood	Yang Earth	Yang Fire	Yin Fire	Yin Earth	Yang Metal	Yin Metal	Yang Earth
Hidden Elements	Yang Wood		Yin Water Yin Metal	Yang Fire Yang Earth		Yin Wood Yin Water	Yang Earth Yang Metal	Yin Earth	Yin Fire Yin Wood	Yang Earth Yang Water		Yin Metal Yin Fire

1978

Find your Day Here	Month Stem	Month Branch	Year Stem	Year Branch	Day	Day	Time
January 6 – February 4	Yin Water	Ox	Yin Fire	Snake	Jan	59	: 43
February 4— March 6	Yang Wood	Tiger	Yang Earth	Horse	Feb	30	12: 27
March 6— April 5	Yin Wood	Rabbit	Yang Earth	Horse	Mar	58	6: 38
April 5— May 6	Yang Fire	Dragon	Yang Earth	Horse	April	29	11: 39
May 6 – June 6	Yin Fire	Snake	Yang Earth	Horse	May	59	5: 09
June 6— July 7	Yang Earth	Horse	Yang Earth	Horse	June	30	9:23
July 7— August 8	Yin Earth	Sheep	Yang Earth	Horse	July	60	19: 37
August 8— September 8	Yang Metal	Monkey	Yang Earth	Horse	Aug	31	5: 18
September 8 – October 8	Yin Metal	Cock	Yang Earth	Horse	Sep	2	8: 03
October 8— November 8	Yang Water	Dog	Yang Earth	Horse	Oct	32	23: 31
November 8— December 7	Yin Water	Pig	Yang Earth	Horse	Nov	3	2: 34
December 7 – January 6	Yang Wood	Rat	Yang Earth	Horse	Dec	33	19: 20

1979

Find your Day Here	Month Stem	Month Branch	Year Stem	Year Branch	Day	Day	Time
January 6 – February 4	Yin Wood	Ox	Yang Earth	Horse	Jan	4	6: 32
February 4— March 6	Yang Fire	Tiger	Yin Earth	Sheep	Feb	35	18: 13
March 6— April 5	Yin Fire	Rabbit	Yin Earth	Sheep	Mar	3	12: 20
April 5— May 6	Yang Earth	Dragon	Yin Earth	Sheep	April	34	17: 18
May 6 – June 6	Yin Earth	Snake	Yin Earth	Sheep	May	4	10: 47
June 6— July 8	Yang Metal	Horse	Yin Earth	Sheep	June	35	15: 05
July 8— August 8	Yin Metal	Sheep	Yin Earth	Sheep	July	5	1: 25
August 8— September 8	Yang Water	Monkey	Yin Earth	Sheep	Aug	36	11: 11
September 8 – October 9	Yin Water	Cock	Yin Earth	Sheep	Sep	7	14: 00
October 9— November 8	Yang Wood	Dog	Yin Earth	Sheep	Oct	37	5: 30
November 8— December 8	Yin Wood	Pig	Yin Earth	Sheep	Nov	8	8: 33
December 8 – January 6	Yang Fire	Rat	Yin Earth	Sheep	Dec	38	1: 18

Branch	Pig	Rat	Ox	Tiger	Rabbit	Dragon	Snake	Horse	Sheep	Monkey	Cock	Dog
Main Element	Yang Water	Yin Water	Yin Earth	Yang Wood	Yin Wood	Yang Earth	Yang Fire	Yin Fire	Yin Earth	Yang Metal	Yin Metal	Yang Earth
Hidden Elements	Yang Wood		Yin Water Yin Metal	Yang Fire Yang Earth		Yin Wood Yin Water	Yang Earth Yang Metal	Yin Earth	Yin Fire Yin Wood	Yang Earth Yang Water		Yin Metal Yin Fire

1980

Find yourDay Here	Month Stem	Month Branch	Year Stem	Year Branch	Day	Day	Time
January 6 – February 5	Yin Fire	Ox	Yin Earth	Sheep	Jan	9	12: 29
February 5 – 29,— March 5	Yang Earth	Tiger	Yang Metal	Monkey	Feb	40	: 10
March 5 – April 4	Yin Earth	Rabbit	Yang Metal	Monkey	Mar	9	18: 17
April 4 – May 5	Yang Metal	Dragon	Yang Metal	Monkey	April	40	23: 15
May 5 – June 5	Yin Metal	Snake	Yang Metal	Monkey	May	10	16: 45
June 5 – July 7	Yang Water	Horse	Yang Metal	Monkey	June	41	21: 04
July 7 – August 7	Yin Water	Sheep	Yang Metal	Monkey	July	11	7: 24
August 7– September 7	Yang Wood	Monkey	Yang Metal	Monkey	Aug	42	17: 09
September 7 – October 8	Yin Wood	Cock	Yang Metal	Monkey	Sep	13	19: 54
October 8 – November 7	Yang Fire	Dog	Yang Metal	Mo nkey	Oct	43	11: 19
November 7 – December 7	Yin Fire	Pig	Yang Metal	Monkey	Nov	14	14: 18
December 7 – January 5	Yang Earth	Rat	Yang Metal	Monkey	Dec	44	7: 02

1981

Find your Day Here	Month Stem	Month Branch	Year Stem	Year Branch	Day	Day	Time
January 5 – February 4	Yin Earth	Ox	Yang Metal	Monkey	Jan	15	18: 13
February 4— March 6	Yang Metal	Tiger	Yin Metal	Cock	Feb	46	5: 56
March 6— April 5	Yin Metal	Rabbit	Yin Metal	Cock	Mar	14	: 05
April 5— May 5	Yang Water	Dragon	Yin Metal	Cock	April	45	5: 05
May 5– June 6	Yin Water	Snake	Yin Metal	Cock	May	15	22: 35
June 6— July 7	Yang Wood	Horse	Yin Metal	Cock	June	46	2: 53
July 7— August 7	Yin Wood	Sheep	Yin Metal	Cock	July	16	13: 12
August 7— September 8	Yang Fire	Monkey	Yin Metal	Cock	Aug	47	22: 57
September 8 – October 8	Yin Fire	Cock	Yin Metal	Cock	Sep	18	1: 43
October 8— November 7	Yang Earth	Dog	Yin Metal	Cock	Oct	48	17: 10
November 7— December 7	Yin Earth	Pig	Yin Metal	Cock	Nov	19	20: 19
December 7 – January 6	Yang Metal	Rat	Yin Metal	Cock	Dec	49	12: 51

	Pig	Rat	Ox	Tiger	Rabbit	Dragon	Snake	Horse	Sheep	Monkey	Cock	Dog
Main Element	Yang Water	Yin Water	Yin Earth	Yang Wood	Yin Wood	Yang Earth	Yang Fire	Yin Fire	Yin Earth	Yang Metal	Yin Metal	Yang Earth
Hidden Elements	Yang Wood		Yin Water Yin Metal	Yang Fire Yang Earth		Yin Wood Yin Water	Yang Earth Yang Metal	Yin Earth	Yin Fire Yin Wood	Yang Earth Yang Water		Yin Metal Yin Fire

1982

Find your Day Here	Month Stem	Month Branch	Year Stem	Year Branch	Day	Day	Time
January 6 – February 4	Yin Metal	Ox	Yin Metal	Cock	Jan	20	: 03
February 4— March 6	Yang Water	Tiger	Yang Water	Dog	Feb	51	11: 46
March 6— April 5	Yin Water	Rabbit	Yang Water	Dog	Mar	19	5: 55
April 5— May 6	Yang Wood	Drag on	Yang Water	Dog	April	50	10: 53
May 6 – June 6	Yin Wood	Snake	Yang Water	Dog	May	20	4: 20
June 6— July 7	Yang Fire	Horse	Yang Water	Dog	June	51	8: 36
July 7— August 8	Yin Fire	Sheep	Yang Water	Dog	July	21	18: 55
August 8— September 8	Yang Earth	Monkey	Yang Water	Dog	Aug	52	4: 42
September 8 – October 8	Yin Earth	Cock	Yang Water	Dog	Sep	23	7: 32
October 8— November 8	Yang Metal	Dog	Yang Water	Dog	Oct	53	23: 02
November 8 - December 7	Yin Metal	Pig	Yang Water	Dog	Nov	24	2: 04
December 7 – January 6	Yang Water	Rat	Yang Water	Dog	Dec	54	18: 48

1983

Find your Day Here	Month Stem	Month Branch	Year Stem	Year Branch	Day	Day	Time
January 6 – February 4	Yin Water	Ox	Yang Water	Dog	Jan	25	5: 59
February 4— March 6	Yang Wood	Tiger	Yin Water	Pig	Feb	56	17: 40
March 6— April 5	Yin Wood	Rabbit	Yin Water	Pig	Mar	24	11: 47
April 5— May 6	Yang Fire	Dragon	Yin Water	Pig	April	55	16: 45
May 6 – June 6	Yin Fire	Snake	Yin Water	Pig	May	25	10: 11
June 6— July 8	Yang Earth	Horse	Yin Water	Pig	June	56	14: 26
July 8— August 8	Yin Earth	Sheep	Yin Water	Pig	July	26	: 43
August 8— September 8	Yang Metal	Monkey	Yin Water	Pig	Aug	57	10: 30
September 8 – October 9	Yin Metal	Cock	Yin Water	Pig	Sep	28	13: 20
October 9— November 8	Yang Water	Dog	Yin Water	Pig	Oct	58	4: 51
November 8— December 8	Yin Water	Pig	Yin Water	Pig	Nov	29	7: 53
December 8 – January 6	Yang Wood	Rat	Yin Water	Pig	Dec	59	: 34

Branch	Pig	Rat	Ox	Tiger	Rabbit	Dragon	Snake	Horse	Sheep	Monkey	Cock	Dog
Main Element	Yang Water	Yin Water	Yin Earth	Yang Wood	Yin Wood	Yang Earth	Yang Fire	Yin Fire	Yin Earth	Yang Metal	Yin Metal	Yang Earth
Hidden Elements	Yang Wood		Yin Water Yin Metal	Yang Fire Yang Earth		Yin Wood Yin Water	Yang Earth Yang Metal	Yin Earth	Yin Fire Yin Wood	Yang Earth Yang Water		Yin Metal Yin Fire

1984

Find your Day Here	Month Stem	Month Branch	Year Stem	Year Branch	Day	Day	Time
January 6 – February 4	Yin Wood	Ox	Yin Water	Pig	Jan	30	11: 41
February 4— 29,—March 5	Yang Fire	Tiger	Yang Wood	Rat	Feb	1	11: 19
March 5 – April 4	Yin Fire	Rabbit	Yang Wood	Rat	Mar	30	17: 25
April 4 – May 5	Yang Earth	Dragon	Yang Wood	Rat	April	1	22: 22
May 5 – June 5	Yin Earth	Snake	Yang Wood	Rat	May	31	15: 51
June 5 – July 7	Yang Metal	Horse	Yang Wood	Rat	June	2	20: 09
July 7 – August 7	Yin Metal	Sheep	Yang Wood	Rat	July	32	6: 29
August 7– September 7	Yang Water	Monkey	Yang Wood	Rat	Aug	3	16: 18
September 7 – October 8	Yin Water	Cock	Yang Wood	Rat	Sep	34	19: 10
October 8 – November 7	Yang Wood	Dog	Yang Wood	Rat	Oct	4	10: 43
November 7 – December 7	Yin Wood	Pig	Yang Wood	Rat	Nov	35	13: 45
December 7 – January 5	Yang Fire	Rat	Yang Wood	Rat	Dec	5	6: 28

1985

Find your Day Here	Month Stem	Month Branch	Year Stem	Year Branch	Day	Day	Time
January 5 – February 4	Yin Fire	Ox	Yang Wood	Rat	Jan	36	17: 35
February 4— March 5	Yang Earth	Tiger	Yin Wood	Ox	Feb	7	5: 12
March 5— April 5	Yin Earth	Rabbit	Yin Wood	Ox	Mar	35	23: 16
April 5— May 5	Yang Metal	Dragon	Yin Wood	Ox	April	6	4: 14
May 5 – June 6	Yin Metal	Snake	Yin Wood	Ox	May	36	21: 43
June 6— July 7	Yang Water	Horse	Yin Wood	Ox	June	7	2: 00
July 7— August 7	Yin Water	Sheep	Yin Wood	Ox	July	37	12: 19
August 7— September 7	Yang Wood	Monkey	Yin Wood	Ox	Aug	8	22: 04
September 8 – October 8	Yin Wood	Cock	Yin Wood	Ox	Sep	39	: 53
October 8— November 7	Yang Fire	Dog	Yin Wood	Ox	Oct	9	16: 24
November 7— December 7	Yin Fire	Pig	Yin Wood	Ox	Nov	40	19: 29
December 7 – January 5	Yang Earth	Rat	Yin Wood	Ox	Dec	10	12: 16

	Pig	Rat	Ox	Tiger	Rabbit	Dragon	Snake	Horse	Sheep	Monkey	Cock	Dog
Main Element	Yang Water	Yin Water	Yin Earth	Yang Wood	Yin Wood	Yang Earth	Yang Fire	Yin Fire	Yin Earth	Yang Metal	Yin Metal	Yang Earth
Hidden Elements	Yang Wood		Yin Water Yin Metal	Yang Fire Yang Earth		Yin Wood Yin Water	Yang Earth Yang Metal	Yin Earth	Yin Fire Yin Wood	Yang Earth Yang Water		Yin Metal Yin Fire

1986

Find your Day Here	Month Stem	Month Branch	Year Stem	Year Branch	Day	Day	Time
January 5 – February 4	Yin Earth	Ox	Yin Wood	Ox	Jan	41	23: 29
February 4— March 6	Yang Metal	Tiger	Yang Fire	Tiger	Feb	12	11: 09
March 6— April 5	Yin Metal	Rabbit	Yang Fire	Tiger	Mar	40	5: 11
April 5— May 6	Yang Water	Dragon	Yang Fire	Tiger	April	11	10: 05
May 6– June 6	Yin Water	Snake	Yang Fire	Tiger	May	41	3: 30
June 6— July 7	Yang Wood	Horse	Yang Fire	Tiger	June	12	7: 44
July 7— August 8	Yin Wood	Sheep	Yang Fire	Tiger	July	42	18: 00
August 8— September 8	Yang Fire	Monkey	Yang Fire	Tiger	Aug	13	3: 52
September 8 – October 8	Yin Fire	Cock	Yang Fire	Tiger	Sep	44	6:34
October 8— November 8	Yang Earth	Dog	Yang Fire	Tiger	Oct	14	22: 08
November 8— December 7	Yin Earth	Pig	Yang Fire	Tiger	Nov	45	1:1 2
December 7 – January 6	Yang Metal	Rat	Yang Fire	Tiger	Dec	15	18: 02

1987

Find your Day Here	Month Stem	Month Branch	Year Stem	Year Branch	Day	Day	Time
January 6 – February 4	Yin Metal	Ox	Yang Fire	Tiger	Jan	46	5: 13
February 4— March 6	Yang Water	Tiger	Yin Fire	Rabbit	Feb	22	16: 52
March 6— April 5	Yin Water	Rabbit	Yin Fire	Rabbit	Mar	45	10: 55
April 5— May 6	Yang Wood	Dragon	Yin Fire	Rabbit	April	16	15: 44
May 6 – June 6	Yin Wood	Snake	Yin Fire	Rabbit	May	46	9: 07
June 6— July 7	Yang Fire	Horse	Yin Fire	Rabbit	June	17	13: 20
July 7— August 8	Yin Fire	Sheep	Yin Fire	Rabbit	July	47	23: 40
August 8— September 8	Yang Earth	Monkey	Yin Fire	Rabbit	Aug	18	9: 30
September 8 – October 9	Yin Earth	Cock	Yin Fire	Rabbit	Sep	49	12: 25
October 9— November 8	Yang Metal	Dog	Yin Fire	Rabbit	Oct	19	3: 59
November 8— December7	Yin Metal	Pig	Yin Fire	Rabbit	Nov	50	7: 05
December 7 – January 6	Yang Water	Rat	Yin Fire	Rabbit	Dec	20	23: 51

Branch	Pig	Rat	Ox	Tiger	Rabbit	Dragon	Snake	Horse	Sheep	Monkey	Cock	Dog
Main Element	Yang Water	Yin Water	Yin Earth	Yang Wood	Yin Wood	Yang Earth	Yang Fire	Yin Fire	Yin Earth	Yang Metal	Yin Metal	Yang Earth
Hidden Elements	Yang Wood		Yin Water Yin Metal	Yang Fire Yang Earth		Yin Wood Yin Water	Yang Earth Yang Metal	Yin Earth	Yin Fire Yin Wood	Yang Earth Yang Water		Yin Metal Yin Fire

1988

	Month		Year				
Find your Day Here	Stem	Branch	Stem	Branch	Day	Day	Time
January 6 – February 4	Yin Water	Ox	Yin Fire	Rabbit	Jan	51	11: 04
February 4 – 29,— March 5	Yang Wood	Tiger	Yang Earth	Dragon	Feb	22	22: 43
March 5— April 4	Yin Wood	Rabbit	Yang Earth	Dragon	Mar	51	16: 46
April 4— May 5	Yang Fire	Dragon	Yang Earth	Dragon	April	22	21: 38
May 5 – June 5	Yin Fire	Snake	Yang Earth	Dragon	May	52	15: 02
June 5— July 7	Yang Earth	Horse	Yang Earth	Dragon	June	23	19: 13
July 7— August 7	Yin Earth	Sheep	Yang Earth	Dragon	July	53	5:33
August 7— September 7	Yang Metal	Monkey	Yang Earth	Dragon	Aug	24	15: 19
September 7 – October 8	Yin Metal	Cock	Yang Earth	Dragon	Sep	55	18: 11
October 8— November 7	Yang Water	Dog	Yang Earth	Dragon	Oct	25	9: 44
November 7— December 7	Yin Water	Pig	Yang Earth	Dragon	Nov	56	12: 48
December 7 – January 5	Yang Wood	Rat	Yang Earth	Dragon	Dec	26	5: 34

1989

	Month		Year				
Find your Day Here	Stem	Branch	Stem	Branch	Day	Day	Time
January 5 – February 4	Yin Wood	Ox	Yang Earth	Dragon	Jan	57	16: 45
February 4— March 5	Yang Fire	Tiger	Yin Earth	Snake	Feb	28	4: 27
March 5— April 5	Yin Fire	Rabbit	Yin Earth	Snake	Mar	56	22: 34
April 5— May 5	Yang Earth	Dragon	Yin Earth	Snake	April	27	3: 30
May 5 – June 6	Yin Earth	Snake	Yin Earth	Snake	May	57	20:54
June 6— July 7	Yang Metal	Horse	Yin Earth	Snake	June	28	1:05
July 7— August 7	Yin Metal	Sheep	Yin Earth	Snake	July	58	11:20
August 7— September 8	Yang Water	Monkey	Yin Earth	Snake	Aug	29	21:05
September 8 – October 8	Yin Water	Cock	Yin Earth	Snake	Sep	60	23: 54
October 8— November 7	Yang Wood	Dog	Yin Earth	Snake	Oct	30	15:28
November 7— December 7	Yin Wood	Pig	Yin Earth	Snake	Nov	1	18: 34
December 7 – January 5	Yang Fire	Rat	Yin Earth	Snake	Dec	31	11: 21

Branch	Pig	Rat	Ox	Tiger	Rabbit	Dragon	Snake	Horse	Sheep	Monkey	Cock	Dog
Main Element	Yang Water	Yin Water	Yin Earth	Yang Wood	Yin Wood	Yang Earth	Yang Fire	Yin Fire	Yin Earth	Yang Metal	Yin Metal	Yang Earth
Hidden Elements	Yang Wood		Yin Water Yin Metal	Yang Fire Yang Earth		Yin Wood Yin Water	Yang Earth Yang Metal	Yin Earth	Yin Fire Yin Wood	Yang Earth Yang Water		Yin Metal Yin Fire

1990

Find your Day Here	Month Stem	Month Branch	Year Stem	Year Branch	Day	Day	Time
January 5 – February 4	Yin Fire	Ox	Yin Earth	Snake	Jan	2	22: 34
February 4— March 6	Yang Earth	Tiger	Yang Metal	Horse	Feb	33	10: 15
March 6— April 5	Yin Earth	Rabbit	Yang Metal	Horse	Mar	1	4: 21
April 5— May 6	Yang Metal	Dragon	Yang Metal	Horse	April	32	9: 14
May 6– June 6	Yin Metal	Snake	Yang Metal	Horse	May	2	2: 34
June 6— July 7	Yang Water	Horse	Yang Metal	Horse	June	33	6: 47
July 7— August 8	Yin Water	Sheep	Yang Metal	Horse	July	3	17: 00
August 8— September 8	Yang Wood	Monkey	Yang Metal	Horse	Aug	34	2: 46
September 8 – October 8	Yin Wood	Cock	Yang Metal	Horse	Sep	5	5: 38
October 8— November 8	Yang Fire	Dog	Yang Metal	Ho rse	Oct	35	21: 13
November 8— December 7	Yin Fire	Pig	Yang Metal	Horse	Nov	6	: 23
December 7 – January 6	Yang Earth	Rat	Yang Metal	Horse	Dec	36	17: 14

1991

Find your Day Here	Month Stem	Month Branch	Year Stem	Year Branch	Day	Day	Time
January 6 – February 4	Yin Earth	Ox	Yang Metal	Horse	Jan	7	4: 28
February 4— March 6	Yang Metal	Tiger	Yin Metal	Sheep	Feb	38	16: 08
March 6— April 5	Yin Metal	Rabbit	Yin Metal	Sheep	Mar	6	10: 13
April 5— May 6	Yang Water	Dragon	Yin Metal	Sheep	April	37	15: 04
May 6 – June 6	Yin Water	Snake	Yin Metal	Sheep	May	7	8: 27
June 6— July 7	Yang Wood	Horse	Yin Metal	Sheep	June	38	12: 37
July 7— August 8	Yin Wood	Sheep	Yin Metal	Sheep	July	8	22: 52
August 8— September 8	Yang Fire	Monkey	Yin Metal	Sheep	Aug	39	8: 36
September 8 – October 9	Yin Fire	Cock	Yin Metal	Sheep	Sep	10	11: 27
October 9— November 8	Yang Ea rth	Dog	Yin Metal	Sheep	Oct	4	3: 01
November 8- December 7	Yin Earth	Pig	Yin Metal	Sheep	Nov	11	6: 08
December 7 – January 6	Yang Metal	Rat	Yin Metal	Sheep	Dec	41	22: 56

Branch	Pig	Rat	Ox	Tiger	Rabbit	Dragon	Snake	Horse	Sheep	Monkey	Cock	Dog
Main Element	Yang Water	Yin Water	Yin Earth	Yang Wood	Yin Wood	Yang Earth	Yang Fire	Yin Fire	Yin Earth	Yang Metal	Yin Metal	Yang Earth
Hidden Elements	Yang Wood		Yin Water Yin Metal	Yang Fire Yang Earth		Yin Wood Yin Water	Yang Earth Yang Metal	Yin Earth	Yin Fire Yin Wood	Yang Earth Yang Water		Yin Metal Yin Fire

1992

Find your Day Here	Month Stem	Month Branch	Year Stem	Year Branch	Day	Day	Time
January 6– February 4	Yin Metal	Ox	Yin Metal	Sheep	Jan	12	10: 09
February 4 – 29,— March 5	Yang Water	Tiger	Yang Water	Monkey	Feb	43	21: 48
March 5— April 4	Yin Water	Rabbit	Yang Water	Monkey	Mar	12	15: 52
April 4— May 5	Yang Wood	Dragon	Yang Water	Monkey	April	43	20: 45
May 5 – June 5	Yin Wood	Snake	Yang Water	Monkey	May	13	14: 09
June 5— July 7	Yang Fire	Horse	Yang Water	Monkey	June	44	18: 24
July 7— August 7	Yin Fire	Sheep	Yang Water	Monkey	July	14	4: 40
August 7— September 7	Yang Earth	Monkey	Yang Water	Monkey	Aug	45	14: 28
September 7 – October 8	Yin Earth	Cock	Yang Water	Monkey	Sep	16	17: 19
October 8— November 7	Yang Metal	Dog	Yang Water	Monkey	Oct	46	8: 52
November 7— December 7	Yin Metal	Pig	Yang Water	Monkey	Nov	17	11: 57
December 7 – January 5	Yang Water	Rat	Yang Water	Monkey	Dec	47	4: 44

1993

Find your Day Here	Month Stem	Month Branch	Year Stem	Year Branch	Day	Day	Time
January 5 – February 4	Yin Water	Ox	Yang Water	Monkey	Jan	18	15: 57
February 4 —March 5	Yang Wood	Tiger	Yin Water	Cock	Feb	49	3: 38
March 5 – April 5	Yin Wood	Rabbit	Yin Water	Cock	Mar	17	21: 42
April 5 – May 5	Yang Fire	Dragon	Yin Water	Cock	April	48	2: 36
May 5 – June 6	Yin Fire	Snake	Yin Water	Cock	May	18	20: 02
June 6 – July 7	Yang Earth	Horse	Yin Water	Cock	June	49	: 15
July 7 – August 7	Yin Earth	Sheep	Yin Water	Cock	July	19	10: 31
August 7– September 7	Yang Metal	Monkey	Yin Water	Cock	Aug	50	20: 17
September 7 – October 8	Yin Metal	Cock	Yin Water	Cock	Sep	21	23: 07
October 8 – November 7	Yang Water	Dog	Yin Water	Cock	Oct	51	14: 41
November 7 – December 8	Yin Water	Pig	Yin Water	Cock	Nov	22	17: 46
December 8 – January 5	Yang Wood	Rat	Yin Water	Cock	Dec	52	10: 33

Branch	Pig	Rat	Ox	Tiger	Rabbit	Dragon	Snake	Horse	Sheep	Monkey	Cock	Dog
Main Element	Yang Water	Yin Water	Yin Earth	Yang Wood	Yin Wood	Yang Earth	Yang Fire	Yin Fire	Yin Earth	Yang Metal	Yin Metal	Yang Earth
Hidden Elements	Yang Wood		Yin Water Yin Metal	Yang Fire Yang Earth		Yin Wood Yin Water	Yang Earth Yang Metal	Yin Earth	Yin Fire Yin Wood	Yang Earth Yang Water		Yin Metal Yin Fire

1994

Find your Day Here	Month Stem	Month Branch	Year Stem	Year Branch	Day	Day	Time
January 5 – February 4	Yin Wood	Ox	Yin Water	Cock	Jan	23	21: 46
February 4— March 6	Yang Fire	Tiger	Yang Wood	Dog	Feb	54	9: 31
March 6— April 5	Yin Fire	Rabbit	Yang Wood	Dog	Mar	22	3: 37
April 5— May 6	Yang Earth	Dragon	Yang Wood	Dog	April	53	8: 31
May 6—June 6	Yin Earth	Snake	Yang Wood	Dog	May	23	1: 54
June 6— July 7	Yang Metal	Horse	Yang Wood	Dog	June	54	6: 05
July 7— August 8	Yin Metal	Sheep	Yang Wood	Dog	July	24	16: 19
August 8— September 7	Yang Water	Monkey	Yang Wood	Dog	Aug	55	2: 05
September 8 – October 8	Yin Water	Cock	Yang Wood	Dog	Sep	26	4: 55
October 8— November 7	Yang Wood	Dog	Yang Wood	Dog	Oct	56	20:30
November 7— December 7	Yin Wood	Pig	Yang Wood	Dog	Nov	27	23: 36
December 7 – January 6	Yang Fire	Rat	Yang Wood	Dog	Dec	57	16: 24

1995

Find your Day Here	Month Stem	Month Branch	Year Stem	Year Branch	Day	Day	Time
January 6 – February 4	Yin Fire	Ox	Yang Wood	Dog	Jan	28	3: 34
February 4— March 6	Yang Earth	Tiger	Yin Wood	Pig	Feb	59	15: 14
March 6— April 6	Yin Earth	Rabbit	Yin Wood	Pig	Mar	27	9: 16
April 6— May 6	Yang Metal	Dragon	Yin Wood	Pig	April	58	14: 09
May 6– June 7	Yin Metal	Snake	Yin Wood	Pig	May	28	7:31
June 7— July 7	Yang Water	Horse	Yin Wood	Pig	June	59	11: 43
July 7— August 8	Yin Water	Sheep	Yin Wood	Pig	July	29	22: 02
August 8— September 8	Yang Wood	Monkey	Yin Wood	Pig	Aug	60	7: 53
September 8 – October 9	Yin Wood	Cock	Yin Wood	Pig	Sep	31	10: 49
October 9— November 8	Yang Fire	Dog	Yin Wood	Pig	Oct	1	2: 27
November 8— December 7	Yin Fire	Pig	Yin Wood	Pig	Nov	32	5: 35
December 7 – January 6	Yang Earth	Rat	Yin Wood	Pig	Dec	2	22: 22

Branch	Pig	Rat	Ox	Tiger	Rabbit	Dragon	Snake	Horse	Sheep	Monkey	Cock	Dog
Main Element	Yang Water	Yin Water	Yin Earth	Yang Wood	Yin Wood	Yang Earth	Yang Fire	Yin Fire	Yin Earth	Yang Metal	Yin Metal	Yang Earth
Hidden Elements	Yang Wood		Yin Water Yin Metal	Yang Fire Yang Earth		Yin Wood Yin Water	Yang Earth Yang Metal	Yin Earth	Yin Fire Yin Wood	Yang Earth Yang Water		Yin Metal Yin Fire

1996

Find your Day Here	Month Stem	Month Branch	Year Stem	Year Branch	Day	Day	Time
January 6 – February 4	Yin Earth	Ox	Yin Wood	Pig	Jan	33	9: 31
February 4 – 29,— March 5	Yang Metal	Tiger	Yang Fire	Rat	Feb	4	21 08
March 5- April 4	Yin Metal	Rabbit	Yang Fire	Rat	Mar	33	15:10
April 4— May 5	Yang Water	Dragon	Yang Fire	Rat	April	4	20: 03
May 5 – June 5	Yin Water	Snake	Yang Fire	Rat	May	34	13: 26
June 5— July 7	Yang Wood	Horse	Yang Fire	Rat	June	5	17: 41
July 7— August 7	Yin Wood	Sheep	Yang Fire	Rat	July	35	4:00
August 7— September 7	Yang Fire	Monkey	Yang Fire	Rat	Aug	6	13: 49
September 7 – October 8	Yin Fire	Cock	Yang Fire	Rat	Sep	37	16: 41
October 8— November 7	Yang Earth	Dog	Yang Fire	Rat	Oct	7	8:18
November 7— December 7	Yin Earth	Pig	Yang Fire	Rat	Nov	38	11: 26
December 7 – January 5	Yang Metal	Rat	Yang Fire	Rat	Dec	8	4: 13

1997

Find your Day Here	Month Stem	Month Branch	Year Stem	Year Branch	Day	Day	Time
January 5 – February 4	Yin Metal	Ox	Yang Fire	Rat	Jan	39	15: 22
February 4 —March 5	Yang Water	Tiger	Yin Fire	Ox	Feb	10	3: 04
March 5 – April 5	Yin Water	Rabbit	Yin Fire	Ox	Mar	38	21: 14
April 5 – May 5	Yang Wood	Dragon	Yin Fire	Ox	April	9	2: 17
May 5 – June 5	Yin Wood	Snake	Yin Fire	Ox	May	39	19: 51
June 5 – July 7	Yang Fire	Horse	Yin Fire	Ox	June	10	: 13
July 7 – August 7	Yin Fire	Sheep	Yin Fire	Ox	July	40	10: 36
August 7– September 7	Yang Earth	Monkey	Yin Fire	Ox	Aug	11	20: 19
September 7 – October 8	Yin Earth	Cock	Yin Fire	Ox	Sep	42	23: 03
October 8 – November 7	Yang Metal	Dog	Yin Fire	Ox	Oct	12	14: 27
November 7 – December 7	Yin Metal	Pig	Yin Fire	Ox	Nov	43	17: 22
December 7 – January 5	Yang Water	Rat	Yin Fire	Ox	Dec	13	10: 02

Branch	Pig	Rat	Ox	Tiger	Rabbit	Dragon	Snake	Horse	Sheep	Monkey	Cock	Dog
Main Element	Yang Water	Yin Water	Yin Earth	Yang Wood	Yin Wood	Yang Earth	Yang Fire	Yin Fire	Yin Earth	Yang Metal	Yin Metal	Yang Earth
Hidden Elements	Yang Wood		Yin Water Yin Metal	Yang Fire Yang Earth		Yin Wood Yin Water	Yang Earth Yang Metal	Yin Earth	Yin Fire Yin Wood	Yang Earth Yang Water		Yin Metal Yin Fire

1998

Find your Day Here	Month Stem	Month Branch	Year Stem	Year Branch	Day	Day	Time
January 5 – February 4	Yin Water	Ox	Yin Fire	Ox	Jan	44	21: 11
February 4— March 6	Yang Wood	Tiger	Yang Earth	Tiger	Feb	15	8: 53
March 6— April 5	Yin Wood	Rabbit	Yang Earth	Tiger	Mar	43	3: 03
April 5— May 6	Yang Fire	Dragon	Yang Earth	Tiger	April	14	8: 06
May 6– June 6	Yin Fire	Snake	Yang Earth	Tiger	May	44	1: 40
June 6— July 7	Yang Earth	Horse	Yang Earth	Tiger	June	15	6: 02
July 7— August 8	Yin Earth	Sheep	Yang Earth	Tiger	July	45	16:25
August 8— September 8	Yang Metal	Monkey	Yang Earth	Tiger	Aug	16	2:08
September 8 – October 8	Yin Metal	Cock	Yang Earth	Tiger	Sep	47	4:52
October 8— November 7	Yang Water	Dog	Yang Earth	Tiger	Oct	17	20:16
November 7— December 7	Yin Water	Pig	Yang Earth	Tiger	Nov	48	23: 11
December 7 – January 6	Yang Wood	Rat	Yang Earth	Tiger	Dec	18	15: 51

1999

Find your Day Here	Month Stem	Month Branch	Year Stem	Year Branch	Day	Day	Time
January 6 – February 4	Yin Wood	Ox	Yang Earth	Tiger	Jan	49	3: 00
February 4— March 6	Yang Fire	Tiger	Yin Earth	Rabbit	Feb	20	14: 42
March 6 —April 5	Yin Fire	Rabbit	Yin Earth	Rabbit	Mar	48	8: 52
April 5— May 6	Yang Earth	Dragon	Yin Earth	Rabbit	April	19	13: 55
May 6 – June 6	Yin Earth	Snake	Yin Earth	Rabbit	May	49	7: 29
June 6— July 7	Yang Metal	Horse	Yin Earth	Rabbit	June	20	11: 51
July 7— August 8	Yin Metal	Sheep	Yin Earth	Rabbit	July	50	22: 14
August 8— September 8	Yang Water	Monkey	Yin Earth	Rabbit	Aug	21	7: 57
September 8 – October 9	Yin Water	Cock	Yin Earth	Rabbit	Sep	52	10: 41
October 9— November 8	Yang Wood	Dog	Yin Earth	Rabbit	Oct	22	2: 05
November 8— December 7	Yin Wood	Pig	Yin Earth	Rabbit	Nov	53	5: 01
December 7 – January 6	Yang Fire	Rat	Yin Earth	Rabbit	Dec	23	21: 14

Branch	Pig	Rat	Ox	Tiger	Rabbit	Dragon	Snake	Horse	Sheep	Monkey	Cock	Dog
Main Element	Yang Water	Yin Water	Yin Earth	Yang Wood	Yin Wood	Yang Earth	Yang Fire	Yin Fire	Yin Earth	Yang Metal	Yin Metal	Yang Earth
Hidden Elements	Yang Wood		Yin Water Yin Metal	Yang Fire Yang Earth		Yin Wood Yin Water	Yang Earth Yang Metal	Yin Earth	Yin Fire Yin Wood	Yang Earth Yang Water		Yin Metal Yin Fire

2000

Find your Day Here	Month Stem	Month Branch	Year Stem	Year Branch	Day	Day	Time
January 6 – February 4	Yin Fire	Ox	Yin Earth	Rabbit	Jan	54	8: 50
February 4 – 29,— March 5	Yang Earth	Tiger	Yang Metal	Dragon	Feb	25	20: 32
March 5— April 4	Yin Earth	Rabbit	Yang Metal	Dragon	Mar	54	14: 42
April 4— May 5	Yang Metal	Dragon	Yang Metal	Dragon	April	25	19: 45
May 5 – June 5	Yin Metal	Snake	Yang Metal	Dragon	May	55	13: 19
June 5— July 7	Yang Water	Horse	Yang Metal	Dragon	June	26	17: 41
July 7— August 7	Yin Water	Sheep	Yang Metal	Dragon	July	56	4: 04
August 7— September 7	Yang Wood	Monkey	Yang Metal	Dragon	Aug	27	13: 36
September 7 – October 8	Yin Wood	Cock	Yang Metal	Dragon	Sep	58	14: 33
October 8— November 7	Yang Fire	Dog	Yang Metal	Dragon	Oct	28	7: 54
November 7— December 7	Yin Fire	Pig	Yang Metal	Dragon	Nov	59	10:49
December 7 – January 5	Yang Earth	Rat	Yang Metal	Dragon	Dec	29	3: 29

2001

Find your Day Here	Month Stem	Month Branch	Year Stem	Year Branch	Day	Day	Time
January 5 – February 4	Yin Earth	Ox	Yang Metal	Dragon	Jan	60	14: 38
February 4 —March 5	Yang Metal	Tiger	Yin Metal	Snake	Feb	31	2: 20
March 5 – April 5	Yin Metal	Rabbit	Yin Metal	Snake	Mar	59	20: 30
April 5 – May 5	Yang Water	Dragon	Yin Metal	Snake	April	30	1: 33
May 5 – June 5	Yin Water	Snake	Yin Metal	Snake	May	60	19: 07
June 5 – July 7	Yang Wood	Horse	Yin Metal	Snake	June	31	23: 29
July 7 – August 7	Yin Wood	Sheep	Yin Metal	Snake	July	1	9: 52
August 7– September 7	Yang Fire	Monkey	Yin Metal	Snake	Aug	32	19: 34
September 7 – October 8	Yin Fire	Cock	Yin Metal	Snake	Sep	3	22: 18
October 8 – November 7	Yang Earth	Dog	Yin Metal	Snake	Oct	33	13: 42
November 7 – December 7	Yin Earth	Pig	Yin Metal	Snake	Nov	4	16: 37
December 7 – January 5	Yang Metal	Rat	Yin Metal	Snake	Dec	34	9: 17

Branch	Pig	Rat	Ox	Tiger	Rabbit	Dragon	Snake	Horse	Sheep	Monkey	Cock	Dog
Main Element	Yang Water	Yin Water	Yin Earth	Yang Wood	Yin Wood	Yang Earth	Yang Fire	Yin Fire	Yin Earth	Yang Metal	Yin Metal	Yang Earth
Hidden Elements	Yang Wood		Yin Water Yin Metal	Yang Fire Yang Earth		Yin Wood Yin Water	Yang Earth Yang Metal	Yin Earth	Yin Fire Yin Wood	Yang Earth Yang Water		Yin Metal Yin Fire

2002

	Month		Year				
Find your Day Here	Stem	Branch	Stem	Branch	Day	Day	Time
January 5 – February 4	Yin Metal	Ox	Yin Metal	Snake	Jan	5	20: 26
February 4— March 6	Yang Water	Tiger	Yang Water	Horse	Feb	36	8: 08
March 6— April 5	Yin Water	Rabbit	Yang Water	Horse	Mar	4	2: 18
April 5— May 6	Yang Wood	D ragon	Yang Water	Horse	April	35	7: 21
May 6– June 6	Yin Wood	Snake	Yang Water	Horse	May	5	: 55
June 6— July 7	Yang Fire	Horse	Yang Water	Horse	June	36	5: 17
July 7— August 8	Yin Fire	Sheep	Yang Water	Horse	July	6	15: 40
August 8— September 8	Yang Earth	Monkey	Yang Water	Horse	Aug	37	1: 23
September 8 – October 8	Yin Earth	Cock	Yang Water	Horse	Sep	8	4: 07
October 8— November 7	Yang Metal	Dog	Yang Water	Horse	Oct	38	19: 31
November 7— December 7	Yin Metal	Pig	Yang Water	Horse	Nov	9	22: 26
December 7 – January 6	Yang Water	Rat	Yang Water	Horse	Dec	39	15: 06

2003

	Month		Year				
Find your Day Here	Stem	Branch	Stem	Branch	Day	Day	Time
January 6 – February 4	Yin Water	Ox	Yang Water	Horse	Jan	10	2: 15
February 4— March 6	Yang Wood	Tiger	Yin Water	Sheep	Feb	41	13: 57
March 6— April 5	Yin Wood	Rabbit	Yin Water	Sheep	Mar	9	8: 07
April 5— May 6	Yang Fire	Dragon	Yin Water	Sheep	April	40	13: 10
May 6 – June 6	Yin Fire	Snake	Yin Water	Sheep	May	10	6: 44
June 6— July 7	Yang Earth	Horse	Yin Water	Sheep	June	41	11: 06
July 7— August 8	Yin Earth	Sheep	Yin Water	Sheep	July	11	21: 29
August 8— September 8	Yang Metal	Monkey	Yin Water	Sheep	Aug	42	7: 12
September 8 – October 9	Yin Metal	Cock	Yin Water	Sheep	Sep	13	9: 56
October 9— November 8	Yang Water	Dog	Yin Water	Sheep	Oct	43	1: 20
November 8— December 7	Yin Water	Pig	Yin Water	Sheep	Nov	14	4: 15
December 7 – January 6	Yang Wood	Rat	Yin Water	Sheep	Dec	44	20: 05

Branch	Pig	Rat	Ox	Tiger	Rabbit	Dragon	Snake	Horse	Sheep	Monkey	Cock	Dog
Main Element	Yang Water	Yin Water	Yin Earth	Yang Wood	Yin Wood	Yang Earth	Yang Fire	Yin Fire	Yin Earth	Yang Metal	Yin Metal	Yang Earth
Hidden Elements	Yang Wood		Yin Water Yin Metal	Yang Fire Yang Earth		Yin Wood Yin Water	Yang Earth Yang Metal	Yin Earth	Yin Fire Yin Wood	Yang Earth Yang Water		Yin Metal Yin Fire

2004

Find your Day Here	Month Stem	Month Branch	Year Stem	Year Branch	Day	Day	Time
January 6 – February 4	Yin Wood	Ox	Yin Water	Sheep	Jan	15	8: 04
February 4-29— March 5	Yang Fire	Tiger	Yang Wood	Monkey	Feb	46	19: 58
March 5— April 4	Yin Fire	Rabbit	Yang Wood	Monkey	Mar	15	13: 57
April 4— May 5	Yang Earth	Dragon	Yang Wood	Monkey	April	46	18: 45
May 5 – June 5	Yin Earth	Snake	Yang Wood	Monkey	May	16	12: 04
June 5— July 7	Yang Metal	Horse	Yang Wood	Monkey	June	47	16: 15
July 7— August 7	Yin Metal	Sheep	Yang Wood	Monkey	July	17	2: 33
August 7— September 7	Yang Water	Monkey	Yang Wood	Monkey	Aug	48	12: 21
September 7 – October 8	Yin Water	Cock	Yang Wood	Monkey	Sep	19	15: 14
October 8— November 7	Yang Wood	Dog	Yang Wood	Monkey	Oct	49	6: 51
November 7— December 7	Yin Wood	Pig	Yang Wood	Monkey	Nov	20	10: 00
December 7 – January 5	Yang Fire	Rat	Yang Wood	Monkey	Dec	50	2: 50

2005

Find your Day Here	Month Stem	Month Branch	Year Stem	Year Branch	Day	Day	Time
January 5 – February 4	Yin Fire	Ox	Yang Wood	Monkey	Jan	21	14: 11
February 4— March 5	Yang Earth	Tiger	Yin Wood	Cock	Feb	52	1: 45
March 5— April 5	Yin Earth	Rabbit	Yin Wood	Cock	Mar	20	19: 59
April 5— May 5	Yang Metal	Dragon	Yin Wood	Cock	April	51	: 36
May 5– June 5	Yin Metal	Snake	Yin Wood	Cock	May	21	17: 33
June 5— July 7	Yang Water	Horse	Yin Wood	Cock	June	52	22: 03
July 7— August 7	Yin Water	Sheep	Yin Wood	Cock	July	22	8: 18
August 7— September 7	Yang Wood	Monkey	Yin Wood	Cock	Aug	53	18: 05
September 7 – October 8	Yin Wood	Cock	Yin Wood	Cock	Sep	24	20: 58
October 8— November 7	Yang Fire	Dog	Yin Wood	Cock	Oct	54	12: 35
November 7— December 7	Yin Fire	Pig	Yin Wood	Cock	Nov	25	15: 44
December 7 – January 5	Yang Earth	Rat	Yin Wood	Cock	Dec	55	8: 34

Branch	Pig	Rat	Ox	Tiger	Rabbit	Dragon	Snake	Horse	Sheep	Monkey	Cock	Dog
Main Element	Yang Water	Yin Water	Yin Earth	Yang Wood	Yin Wood	Yang Earth	Yang Fire	Yin Fire	Yin Earth	Yang Metal	Yin Metal	Yang Earth
Hidden Elements	Yang Wood		Yin Water Yin Metal	Yang Fire Yang Earth		Yin Wood Yin Water	Yang Earth Yang Metal	Yin Earth	Yin Fire Yin Wood	Yang Earth Yang Water		Yin Metal Yin Fire

2006

Find your Day Here	Month Stem	Month Branch	Year Stem	Year Branch	Day	Day	Time
January 5 – February 4	Yin Earth	Ox	Yin Wood	Cock	Jan	26	19: 49
February 4— March 6	Yang Metal	Tiger	Yang Fire	Dog	Feb	57	7: 29
March 6— April 5	Yin Metal	Rabbit	Yang Fire	Dog	Mar	25	1: 30
April 5— May 5	Yang Water	Dragon	Yang Fire	Dog	April	56	6: 17
May 5– June 6	Yin Water	Snake	Yang Fire	Dog	May	26	23: 32
June 6— July 7	Yang Wood	Horse	Yang Fire	Dog	June	57	3: 38
July 7— August 8	Yin Wood	Sheep	Yang Fire	Dog	July	27	13: 53
August 8— September 8	Yang Fire	Monkey	Yang Fire	Dog	Aug	58	23: 42
September 8 – October 8	Yin Fire	Cock	Yang Fire	Dog	Sep	29	2: 40
October 8— November 7	Yang Earth	Dog	Yang Fire	Dog	Oct	59	18: 23
November 7— December 7	Yin Earth	Pig	Yang Fire	Dog	Nov	30	21: 36
December 7 – January 6	Yang Metal	Rat	Yang Fire	Dog	Dec	60	14: 28

2007

Find your Day Here	Month Stem	Month Branch	Year Stem	Year Branch	Day	Day	Time
January 6 – February 4	Yin Metal	Ox	Yang Fire	Dog	Jan	31	1: 42
February 4— March 6	Yang Water	Tiger	Yin Fire	Pig	Feb	2	13: 20
March 6— April 5	Yin Water	Rabbit	Yin Fire	Pig	Mar	30	7:19
April 5— May 6	Yang Wood	D ragon	Yin Fire	Pig	April	1	12: 06
May 6– June 6	Yin Wood	Snake	Yin Fire	Pig	May	31	5:21
June 6— July 7	Yang Fire	Horse	Yin Fire	Pig	June	2	9: 28
July 7— August 8	Yin Fire	Sheep	Yin Fire	Pig	July	32	19: 43
August 8— September 8	Yang Earth	Monkey	Yin Fire	Pig	Aug	3	5: 33
September 8 – October 9	Yin Earth	Cock	Yin Fire	Pig	Sep	34	8: 31
October 9— November 8	Yang Metal	Dog	Yin Fire	Pig	Oct	4	: 13
November 8— December 7	Yin Metal	Pig	Yin Fire	Pig	Nov	35	3: 25
December 7 – January 6	Yang Water	Rat	Yin Fire	Pig	Dec	5	20: 16

Branch	Pig	Rat	Ox	Tiger	Rabbit	Dragon	Snake	Horse	Sheep	Monkey	Cock	Dog
Main Element	Yang Water	Yin Water	Yin Earth	Yang Wood	Yin Wood	Yang Earth	Yang Fire	Yin Fire	Yin Earth	Yang Metal	Yin Metal	Yang Earth
Hidden Elements	Yang Wood		Yin Water Yin Metal	Yang Fire Yang Earth		Yin Wood Yin Water	Yang Earth Yang Metal	Yin Earth	Yin Fire Yin Wood	Yang Earth Yang Water		Yin Metal Yin Fire

2008

	Month		Year				
Find your Day Here	Stem	Branch	Stem	Branch	Day	Day	Time
January 6 – February 4	Yin Water	Ox	Yin Fire	Pig	Jan	36	7: 26
February 4-29— March 5	Yang Wood	Tiger	Yang Earth	Rat	Feb	7	19: 02
March 5— April 4	Yin Wood	Rabbit	Yang Earth	Rat	Mar	36	13: 00
April 4— May 5	Yang Fire	Dragon	Yang Earth	Rat	April	7	17: 47
May 5 – June 5	Yin Fire	Snake	Yang Earth	Rat	May	37	11: 05
June 5— July 7	Yang Earth	Horse	Yang Earth	Rat	June	8	15: 13
July 7— August 7	Yin Earth	She ep	Yang Earth	Rat	July	38	1:29
August 7— September 7	Yang Metal	Monkey	Yang Earth	Rat	Aug	9	11: 17
September 7 – October 8	Yin Metal	Cock	Yang Earth	Rat	Sep	40	14: 15
October 8— November 7	Yang Water	Dog	Yang Earth	Rat	Oct	10	6: 02
November 7— December 7	Yin Water	Pig	Yang Earth	Rat	Nov	41	9: 12
December 7 – January 5	Yang Wood	Rat	Yang Earth	Rat	Dec	11	1: 44

2009

	Month		Year				
Find your Day Here	Stem	Branch	Stem	Branch	Day	Day	Time
January 5 – February 4	Yin Wood	Ox	Yang Earth	Rat	Jan	42	13: 16
February 4— March 5	Yang Fire	Tiger	Yin Earth	Ox	Feb	13	: 51
March 5— April 4	Yin Fire	Rabbit	Yin Earth	Ox	Mar	41	18: 49
April 4— May 5	Yang Earth	Dragon	Yin Earth	Ox	April	12	23: 35
May 5– June 5	Yin Earth	Snake	Yin Earth	Ox	May	42	16: 52
June 5— July 7	Yang Metal	Horse	Yin Earth	Ox	June	13	21: 00
July 7— August 7	Yin Metal	Sheep	Yin Earth	Ox	July	43	7: 15
August 7— September 7	Yang Water	Monkey	Yin Earth	Ox	Aug	14	17: 02
September 7 – October 8	Yin Water	Cock	Yin Earth	Ox	Sep	45	19: 59
October 8— November 7	Yang Wood	Dog	Yin Earth	Ox	Oct	15	11: 42
November 7— December 7	Yin Wood	Pig	Yin Earth	Ox	Nov	46	14: 58
December 7 – January 5	Yang Fire	Rat	Yin Earth	Ox	Dec	16	7: 54

Branch	Pig	Rat	Ox	Tiger	Rabbit	Dragon	Snake	Horse	Sheep	Monkey	Cock	Dog
Main Element	Yang Water	Yin Water	Yin Earth	Yang Wood	Yin Wood	Yang Earth	Yang Fire	Yin Fire	Yin Earth	Yang Metal	Yin Metal	Yang Earth
Hidden Elements	Yang Wood		Yin Water Yin Metal	Yang Fire Yang Earth		Yin Wood Yin Water	Yang Earth Yang Metal	Yin Earth	Yin Fire Yin Wood	Yang Earth Yang Water		Yin Metal Yin Fire

2010

Find your Day Here	Month Stem	Month Branch	Year Stem	Year Branch	Day	Day	Time
January 5 – February 4	Yin Fire	Ox	Yin Earth	Ox	Jan	47	19: 10
February 4— March 6	Yang Earth	Tiger	Yang Metal	Tiger	Feb	18	6: 49
March 6— April 5	Yin Earth	Rabbit	Yang Metal	Tiger	Mar	46	1: 48
April 5— May 5	Yang Metal	Dragon	Yang Metal	Tiger	April	17	5: 32
May 5– June 6	Yin Metal	Snake	Yang Metal	Tiger	May	47	22: 45
June 6— July 7	Yang Water	Horse	Yang Metal	Tiger	June	18	2: 51
July 7— August 7	Yin Water	Sheep	Yang Metal	Tiger	July	48	13: 04
August 7— September 8	Yang Wood	Monkey	Yang Metal	Tiger	Aug	19	22: 50
September 8 – October 8	Yin Wood	Cock	Yang Metal	Tiger	Sep	50	1: 46
October 8— November 7	Yang Fire	Dog	Yang Metal	T iger	Oct	20	17: 28
November 7— December 7	Yin Fire	Pig	Yang Metal	Tiger	Nov	51	20: 44
December 7 – January 6	Yang Earth	Rat	Yang Metal	Tiger	Dec	21	13: 40

Branch	Pig	Rat	Ox	Tiger	Rabbit	Dragon	Snake	Horse	Sheep	Monkey	Cock	Dog
Main Element	Yang Water	Yin Water	Yin Earth	Yang Wood	Yin Wood	Yang Earth	Yang Fire	Yin Fire	Yin Earth	Yang Metal	Yin Metal	Yang Earth
Hidden Elements	Yang Wood		Yin Water Yin Metal	Yang Fire Yang Earth		Yin Wood Yin Water	Yang Earth Yang Metal	Yin Earth	Yin Fire Yin Wood	Yang Earth Yang Water		Yin Metal Yin Fire

Printed in the United Kingdom
by Lightning Source UK Ltd.
102416UKS00001B/169

9 780595 174973